Rebound 2004

# Learning Centers
# for
# Young Children

### IDEAS and TECHNIQUES for the
### ELEMENTARY SCHOOL CLASSROOM

GEORGE W. MAXIM

*Hart Publishing Company, Inc.* ● *New York City*

*To Libby Maxim,*
*Rose and Stanley Maxim, Sr.*

GRATEFUL APPRECIATION TO:

The author's wife, Libby. Her compassionate
sacrifices lent the support for this project.

The author's family. Without their willing
support, this project would have remained only
a dream.

Sharyn Flaherty and Rae Ricciuti, who typed
the manuscript. Their outstanding skill and
patience are commendable.

# CONTENTS

Fork, Grow, House, Invisible Ink, Jet
Plane, Knock, Leaves, Magnet, Nail, Oil,
Pennies, Quarter, Ring, Salt Water,
Tacks, Under, Vibrate, Water,
Xylophone, Yourself, Zig-Zag

# INTRODUCTION

There does not seem to be one common definition today which explains the term "learning center." Perhaps a major reason for this problem of definition is that learning centers are primarily designed to meet personal needs of children in highly unique ways. Because of this personalized characteristic, learning centers differ from one another in much the same way that children do, and it is as difficult to describe a typical learning center as it is to describe a typical child.

As they apply to the ideas presented in this book, learning centers will be defined as activities which organize individualized instruction in ways that encourage students to assume major responsibility for their own learning. This means that any independent activity in which the students provide major direction for their own learning is considered a learning center.

An individualized environment which encourages the use of diversified materials and activities to meet individual needs, interests, and abilities should reflect the following beliefs about children and about how they learn:

1. Children are naturally curious and are eager to explore their environment.

2. Learning is not done "to the child" but "by the child."

3. Active exploration and manipulation enhance learning.

4. Play is the child's form of work.

5. Children have both the ability and the initiative to make certain decisions regarding their own learning.

6. Children learn and develop according to their own unique rates and styles.

7. Learning occurs best as it proceeds from the concrete to the abstract.

8. Most facets of an individual's learning are best evaluated through the direct observation of a child at work rather than through paper-pencil tests.

9. Learning to interact and cooperate as a group member is essential to the growth of an individual.

Just subscribing to these beliefs and attitudes does not necessarily guarantee the implementation of an individualized learning-centered classroom. However, such ideas are a necessary underlying component of such classroom organization. By applying these beliefs to the construction of attractive learning centers, the teacher creates a total learning environment that supports the development of each child as an individual.

The educational literature abounds with explanations of individualized or open-concept approaches telling why they are desirable for today's children. The purpose of this book is not to rehash what has been amply covered elsewhere. The author is convinced that practicing teachers are familiar with the injustices that have been described as existing in our nation's schools and possess a fundamental understanding of the theory underlying the remedies which have been proposed as alternatives. In this book the author wishes to present a model or guide which will serve to help teachers implement these changes in the classroom in a painless and organized way. This book is designed as a practical sourcebook to aid teachers as they begin to move toward creating classroom environments which reflect a more individualized setting.

The book is divided into three sections. Section I will focus on a description of the special features of learning centers that make them uniquely designed to meet individual needs. Section II, by far the largest portion of the book, presents blueprints for over one hundred creative learning center activities which have been used successfully in a wide variety of classrooms with children between the ages of five and thirteen. Section III provides specific techniques and suggestions about how to organize and structure the classroom for individualized learning using the learning center format. Thus, this book tries to present the whys, the hows, and especially, the whats of learning centers.

The activities and techniques presented in this book reflect a step-by-step approach to changing the classroom setting. However this sequence need not be followed slavishly. It is the author's intention to encourage teachers to choose those elements which are most appropriate to their students' needs and interests, and to adapt or ignore those which do not adequately meet the children's individual needs. It is hoped that teachers will find this book a stimulant and will begin to innovate and create elaborations or new forms as the need arises.

The author feels strongly that the learning center approach to individualized, open-concept teaching greatly enriched his own elementary school teaching experiences. Sharing his ideas and techniques with teachers through college workshops and varied in-service activities, he encountered an enthusiastic response and received many requests to have the ideas written down in order that concrete reminders might be retained once the displays were gone. The result is this book, which seeks to make available to all teachers a practical idea bank related to learning centers and their organization.

# Learning Centers
## for
## Young Children

# SECTION I

# LEARNING CENTERS:
## Characteristics and Purposes

### Features of Learning Centers

May I invite you to close your eyes for a moment and travel back to that wonderful time in your life which was filled with fantasy and imagination. Reach back and recall some of the exciting experiences of your childhood—that vital period of life which should be preserved and valued as an important component of the personality of every teacher. Riffle through memories of bubble gum, playground swings, scraped knees, a favorite pet . . . and the time an adventure led to a secret corner of a dark closet which concealed a brightly wrapped gift package meant especially for your special day! "I think I know what's in the box—but could it really be . . . ? I just can't wait to open it up and see the exciting surprise waiting just for me!"

Anticipating what the classroom environment will contain should be just as exciting for the young child as guessing the contents of a gift package. The experiences and adventures in store should be so interesting as to produce intensive anticipation and the desire for extensive personal involvement in the challenging projects available.

All too often, it doesn't take long for the child's feeling of exquisite anticipation to be squelched by the typical uninspired classroom experiences. If you are the kind of teacher who would like to preserve and nourish the child's natural curiosity and joy, you are invited to read along and share in the suggestions which have helped numbers of teachers create exciting classroom environments through initiating the learning center approach.

### Definition

A learning center is an area in which organized learning materials motivate and enable children to assume individual responsibility for their own learning.

"FOR WHAT PURPOSE COULD I USE
LEARNING CENTERS WITH MY STUDENTS?"

## Types of Learning Centers

Learning centers can serve to meet most or all of the normal instructional purposes of the classroom. Teachers have successfully used learning centers for one or a combination of the following reasons:

1. *To reinforce learning which had previously been introduced through other teaching techniques.* You may designate a special corner of the room as a place where children may go to independently pursue follow-up activities designed to reinforce learning introduced through teacher-taught group lessons.

2. *To introduce new learnings.* You may design creative independent activities which the children use in place of conventional teacher-directed assignments to develop new concepts, skills, or attitudes.

3. *To enrich or extend learnings and interests.* You may wish to enrich students' understandings of concepts, skills, or attitudes by providing opportunities for them to move beyond what has been learned to explore new and challenging activities.

4. *To stimulate and encourage creativity.* You may want to provide independent experiences which motivate children to generate unique products or ideas. A creativity center should reflect the child's innovation, individuality, and rich imagination.

Here are some specific examples of ways that teachers have used learning centers:

---

**REINFORCEMENT CENTER**

Teacher A wanted his students to have many follow-up experiences with subtraction after he introduced the technique to the entire class. He designed independent learning

---

activities which provided additional practice using subtraction. For example, for one activity the teacher numbered the sides of two foam rubber cubes one through six and four through nine with magic marker. The children rolled the cubes and subtracted the resulting numbers.

## ENRICHMENT CENTER OR CREATIVITY CENTER

Teacher B wished to deepen the interest of her students in poetry as an expressive medium. She introduced several forms of Japanese poetry to the class. They enjoyed interpreting the ideas and the techniques of each form. Then the teacher planned an independent learning center. She displayed pictures of scenic beauty and encouraged the children to compose Haikus or Tankas about them. The children drew their own illustrations for their poems and hung their finished products in the center.

## NEW LEARNING CENTER

Teacher C wanted his pupils to explore on their own the advantages and disadvantages of working individually versus working cooperatively at different kinds of jobs. He set up a center which instructed students to perform a variety of tasks—such as: erasing the chalkboard, illustrating a story, drawing a picture, moving a desk, etc.—first alone, then with another classmate. They first recorded how long it took to complete different tasks by themselves, and then with the help of a partner. Then they shared their reactions and conclusions with each other.

"HOW DO I MAKE
A LEARNING CENTER?"

## Suggestions for Constructing Learning Centers

Once you have decided upon the purpose or purposes of a learning center, consider the following features in your planning:

1. *Analyze your pupils' needs and interests.* Direct observation of children at work or play will probably be the most effective means of finding out what your youngsters are all about. Add to this some simple pretesting techniques (such as your own tests, or standardized tests, skills analysis check lists, or attitude surveys), along with careful consideration of the children's cumulative records. This should provide a suitable basis for determining your childrens' needs and interests. Of major importance is the direct feedback from children in terms of their reactions to the materials you select for use in each learning center.

2. *Choose attractive activities and materials which effectively meet the individual needs and interests of your students.* The following suggestions may be helpful in designing activities and materials for your classroom learning centers:

A. Children prefer activities which are manipulative. Some common devices for making your center activities manipulative are:

## CLOTHESPIN ACTIVITIES

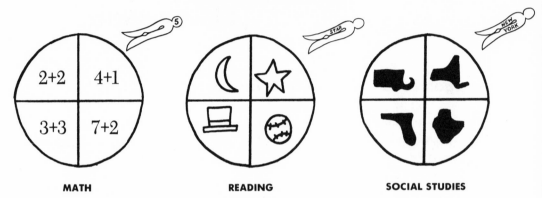

MATH                    READING                    SOCIAL STUDIES

## CAN, MILK CARTON, OR BOX ACTIVITIES

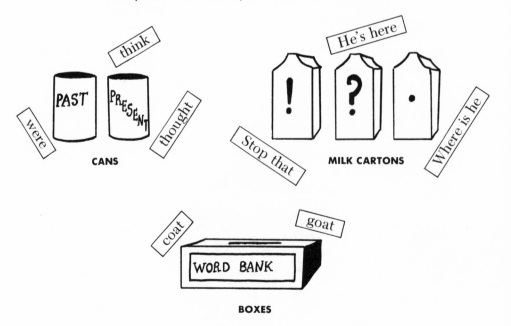

CANS          MILK CARTONS

BOXES

## POCKET CHART ACTIVITIES

## WHEEL ACTIVITIES

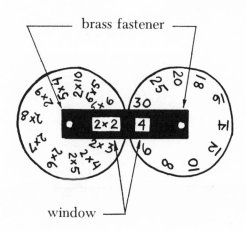

## PUZZLE CARD ACTIVITIES

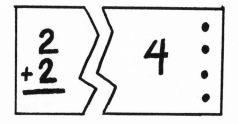

## LACING ACTIVITIES

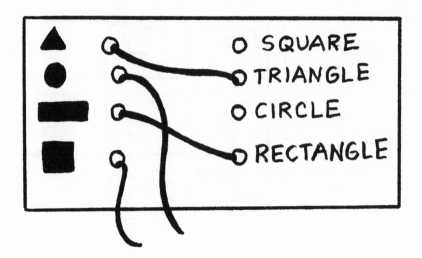

## MISCELLANEOUS MATCHING, SEQUENCING, AND CATEGORIZING ACTIVITIES

**PLACE PICTURES IN SEQUENCE**

**PLACE IN ALPHABETICAL ORDER**

**MATCH ARTICLES AND HEADLINES**

B. *Game boards* greatly stimulate children to learn. Teachers frequently comment on how much children enjoy using center activities which are game oriented. Games give children the same practice they get through drill, but in a more enjoyable form. After using a game board in a spelling center, a child was heard to comment, "I got a perfect paper this week and I didn't even study!"

Game boards are generally used in reinforcement centers, since they involve activities that promote refinement of previously taught ideas or skills. Before constructing a game board, you must carefully evaluate the achievement levels within the class with respect to that particular skill. The game must be designed so that it is neither too hard nor too easy, but gives children a chance to improve a skill in which they are developing proficiency. If the game is too easy, there probably was no point in having it since there was no need for practice in that skill (unless the purpose was to build independence or self-confidence). If the game is too hard, it will be frustrating, and constant failure will kill the children's motivation. Ideally, a game should be so designed that winning or losing depends on the children's ability to use effective strategy to contend with the vagaries of chance. When games combine luck and skill they keep competitiveness in balance; while motivating children to use their best skills, they also allow children to accept defeat graciously and realistically.

There are literally thousands of different ways that game boards may be designed. A few basic formats that seem to be exceptionally popular with young children are given here. Each of these boards can be used for any subject area within the curriculum. (The sample boards illustrated on pages 34 and 35 would each be designed by the teacher to suit the particular subject.) The teacher may print the tasks on the game board squares, or the teacher may prepare a deck of cards with content questions or skills activities printed on them. For example, the cards may require the child to spell, or to identify initial consonant sounds of words pictured, or to furnish synonyms or antonyms for given words, or to add or subtract numbers, and so on.

WHAT'S THE

OPPOSITE OF SHOUT?

To differentiate between easier and harder tasks the teacher may choose to have the card specify the number of spaces to be moved by the player.

WHICH IS LARGER

1/3 OR 1/4?

Check your answer
on the back. If
correct, move ahead
2 spaces.

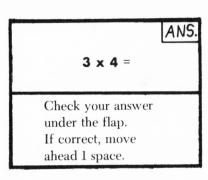

ANS.

3 x 4 =

Check your answer
under the flap.
If correct, move
ahead 1 space.

Other times, this may be left to chance, and spinners or dice may be used to determine the number of spaces to be moved. For example, the child would roll a die and draw a card from a deck. If the child can do successfully what the card asks, he gets to move the number of spaces shown on the die. If he can't, the card is placed at the bottom of the deck and the child must remain where he was until his next move. The game continues until one player reaches the finishing point. In this way, that child, or another player, may get a chance to remember the right answer for the missed question if it comes up again later on.

One suggestion that may help sustain interest in game boards is to include reward and punishment cards as well as skill cards in the deck. For example, an automobile race game board may contain cards such as these:

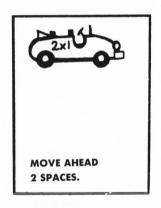

MOVE AHEAD
2 SPACES.

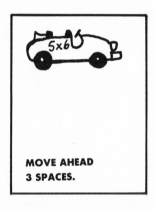

MOVE AHEAD
3 SPACES.

OUT OF GAS—
LOSE ONE TURN.

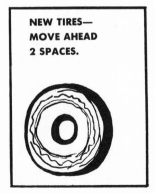

NEW TIRES—
MOVE AHEAD
2 SPACES.

## START-FINISH GAME BOARDS

**AUTOMOBILE RACETRACK**

**MAGNETIC GAME BOARD**

First auto to the finish line is the winner.

First magnetized squirrel to climb the metal washers and reach the top of the tree is the winner.

Hundreds of start-finish game board ideas are possible for the imaginative teacher. How many can you add to this list?

Reach a pot of gold at the end of a rainbow.

Have your cat catch the mouse.

Shoot your rocket to the moon.

Have your magnetized ladybug climb the stem and reach the flower.

## SPORTS GAME BOARDS

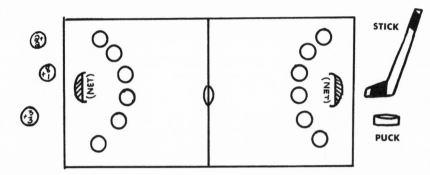

Hockey

Make a large gameboard (24" x 36") in the form of a hockey rink. Draw six circles in a semicircle on each playing side of the board. Get miniature goal nets, hockey sticks, and pucks from a sporting goods or variety store. Using colored construction paper, cut out circles and write a question, problem, or task on each circle. Children take turns choosing a circle and doing what it says. If they are correct, they place the question circle on one of the circles on their side of the board and use the miniature stick and puck to take a shot at the goal. Play continues until a player covers all six circles.

Basketball

Children start at the bottom circle. They take turns drawing cards, and move ahead if they answer the question on the card correctly. They score one point when they move through the basket. Then they continue around again, until one player scores five points.

The same basic format can be followed to design game boards for soccer, football, baseball, tennis, volleyball, or other popular sports. Questions or tasks may be printed right in the circles or squares on the board, in which case the game has a limited life span. Or, the teacher may write rewards and punishments right on the board and put questions and tasks on separate cards which can be changed as needed.

## FAMILIAR GAME BOARDS

### Tic-Tac-Toe

This format can be used for any subject area if the teacher makes up cards with appropriate questions or tasks. Make a large tic-tac-toe board and laminate it so it can be wiped clean after each game. The player selects a card from the deck and performs the task required. If correct, he places an X or O on the board. If incorrect, the play goes to the opponent, who draws a card and attempts to answer correctly. The winner is deternined in the usual way.

### Bingo

| boy | wagon | girl | apple | book |
|-------|-------|------|--------|-------|
| house | box | star | sleep | sun |
| car | dog | FREE | coat | belt |
| mouse | wall | run | horse | glass |
| ball | fork | cup | gloves | cat |

This game may be adapted for different subjects. Each player has a card. Each card is different, but many of the same items appear on some of the cards. The caller (the teacher, an aide, a student) chooses a card from the deck and shows or says what the task is. It may be a math problem; it may be a picture to be matched with a word, as in the sample here; it may be a city to be matched with a country, and so on. Players who have the designated answer on their cards cover up that square with a marker. The first player to complete a row horizontally, vertically, or diagonally wins.

## Checkers

| 2+2 |     | 6+5 |     | 4+8 |     | 6+6 |     |
|-----|-----|-----|-----|-----|-----|-----|-----|
|     | 4+1 |     | 8+6 |     | 6+4 |     | 5+5 |
| 5+3 |     | 7+3 |     | 7+4 |     | 4+4 |     |
|     | 1+1 |     | 5+7 |     | 9+1 |     | 3+3 |
| 9+4 |     | 3+8 |     | 9+7 |     | 4+3 |     |
|     | 8+2 |     | 2+5 |     | 3+1 |     | 8+5 |
| 3+9 |     | 4+5 |     | 8+7 |     | 7+6 |     |
|     | 7+7 |     | 6+9 |     | 2+9 |     | 8+8 |

Children play checkers in the normal way, but they cannot move to another space or jump another player unless a word can be read or spelled, or a math problem done correctly on the space they will land on.

C. Appealing activities with *concrete materials* (realia) can provide exciting learning experiences for children.

EXPERIMENTING

INTERVIEWING

CONSTRUCTING

ILLUSTRATING

HOW MANY BEANS IN THE BOTTLE?

ESTIMATING

COLLECTING DATA

D. Centers may utilize a wide variety of *audio-visual materials* to accomplish specific learning center purposes. The use of tape recorders, films, television, records, film loops, instructional kits, etc., may at times be the most appropriate means of presenting, reinforcing, or enriching a concept. Children enjoy working with learning center materials such as these and, given proper instruction and gui-

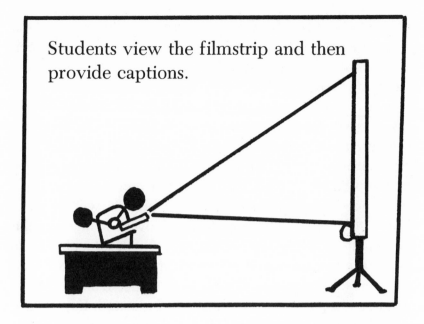

Students view the filmstrip and then provide captions.

dance, soon can be trusted to use the machines independently.

E. Imaginative teachers have created interest and enthusiasm among their children by designing novel independent *written activities.*

Sample surprise cards:

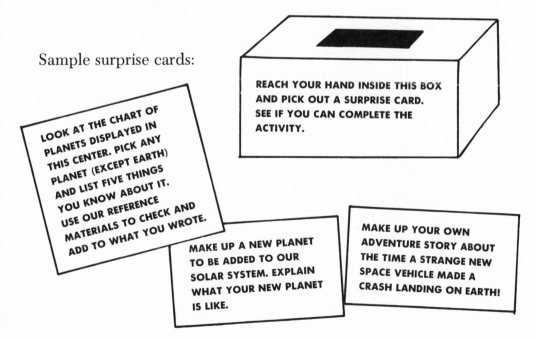

REACH YOUR HAND INSIDE THIS BOX AND PICK OUT A SURPRISE CARD. SEE IF YOU CAN COMPLETE THE ACTIVITY.

LOOK AT THE CHART OF PLANETS DISPLAYED IN THIS CENTER. PICK ANY PLANET (EXCEPT EARTH) AND LIST FIVE THINGS YOU KNOW ABOUT IT. USE OUR REFERENCE MATERIALS TO CHECK AND ADD TO WHAT YOU WROTE.

MAKE UP A NEW PLANET TO BE ADDED TO OUR SOLAR SYSTEM. EXPLAIN WHAT YOUR NEW PLANET IS LIKE.

MAKE UP YOUR OWN ADVENTURE STORY ABOUT THE TIME A STRANGE NEW SPACE VEHICLE MADE A CRASH LANDING ON EARTH!

F. Don't be afraid to use *commercially prepared materials* in your learning centers. Many good learning center games and activities are now being marketed—take advantage of them.

3. *Provide the most appropriate number of activities for the learning center.* Sometimes one activity will be sufficient to meet the purposes of the center, while at other times several activities will be needed. The particular content, as well as the special needs and interests of your students, will dictate the number you will need to provide. Don't overwhelm the children by planning more than they can handle. On the other hand, don't provide them with such unattractive or unchallenging activities that interest in the center will soon wane. Don't hesitate to change or drop an activity if it seems indicated. Experience in using a learning center approach and observing children at work in centers will give insight into what constitutes an appropriate number and variety of activities.

4. *Build into the learning center some means or device so that the children know immediately whether or not a task has been successfully completed.*

A. Provide a special answer key at the center for immediate reference. Or, place the answers on the reverse side of the activity card.

ACTIVITY CARDS

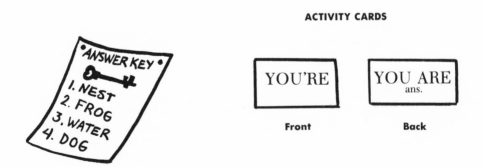

B. Use a code:

● Letter or numeral codes. Letters or numerals are placed on the reverse side of the activity cards, and matching symbols are placed on the bottoms of cans, cartons, or boxes into which the cards are to be sorted. The children know if they are correct when the numerals or letters on the cards and containers match. For example, the children may be sorting words with long a (can 1) or short a (can 2); or they may be sorting words according to whether they have two syllables (can A) or three syllables (can B).

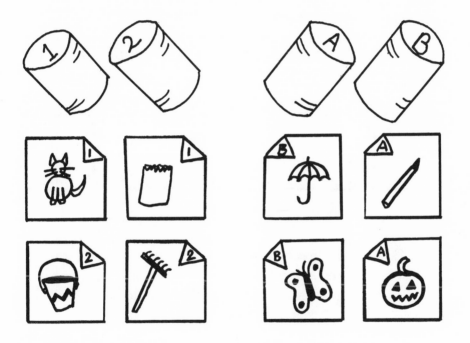

● Symbol or color codes. The same procedure would be used here, except that children would match colors or pictures to check their answers.

C. Include concealed answers. Flaps may be used to cover the answers. Children write their answers in the blanks, and then check their work by folding back the flaps to find the concealed answers.

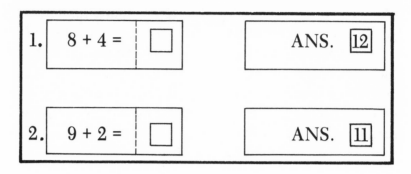

D. Some activities are self-correcting by design. For example, when puzzle pieces fit together, they show the student he is correct.

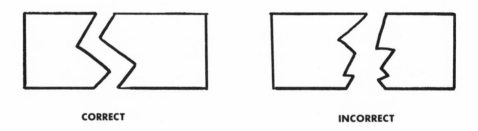

CORRECT                                         INCORRECT

E. Center directors may correct the children's work. Teacher's aides, parent volunteers, older students, or classmates who have completed the activity could be used for this purpose.

F. Teacher-student conferences are often used in addition to self-evaluation. These conferences are especially useful when feedback is needed for creative activities where no one correct answer is expected, or when the teacher wishes to know more about the attitudes of the children toward the activities in the centers. Of course, diagnostic information about the child's growth in skill or concept development also can be acquired as the teacher asks questions or observes pupil performance in activities.

5. *Provide clear directions which will enable your children to use the learning center activities independently.* In addition to carefully introducing the children to each center activity and thoroughly explaining how it should be used, clear directions should be displayed so that the children will be constantly aware of the center's organizational pattern and can function independently. The following suggestions may be helpful in writing directions:

A. Carefully print or type the directions so that they are pleasing to the eye and can be easily seen.

B. Be economical with your words. The basic nature of a learning center requires that children work independently. Therefore, make sure that the vocabulary can be understood by all children. Avoid unnecessary words. For example, don't say, "Get some crayons. Find the stack of drawing paper. Take a piece of paper and draw a winter scene." Instead, "Draw a winter scene," would be much simpler and more easily read by the child. The materials should be provided right at the center.

C. Underline or highlight key words which are essential for the completion of an activity. For example, "*Draw* a picture of . . . "

D. Whenever possible, use action words to begin directions. For example, "*Look* carefully at the picture . . . "

E. Enumerate the directions in proper sequence. For example, "First, ask fifteen classmates to name their favorite rock stars. Second, list the names of the stars in order so that the most popular star is first, etc. Third, compare your list with one of your classmate's list. Are your lists the same or different? Why do you think this is so?"

F. Include pictures or hand-drawn illustrations to help students who may have difficulty reading printed directions.

For example, this symbol  may be used to illustrate a writing task; for a cutting task, and so on.

G. Record the learning center directions on sound tape for the very young child, or for the child who may have extreme reading difficulties.

H. Providing examples in the directions is helpful.

Write two words that are homonyms and draw a picture for each word.
    *Example:*

How many more homonym pairs can you think of?
Show your words to a friend.

I. Whenever possible try to make the directions open-ended. That is, encourage the child to extend the activity into a new area of interest—"How would the results be different if . . ." or "Compare your results with a friend. Why are they the same? Different?"

J. Explain in the directions how the finished work is to be evaluated—an answer key? answers on the reverse side of the material? covered answers?

K. Tell what is to be done with the finished work.

6. *Create an attractive background display for your learning center.* Children respond very favorably to unique packaging techniques. Capitalize on this by providing a colorful background picture accompanied by a catchy caption to attract attention. Place the directions in a strategic spot on the center background.

If you are not a great artist yourself, don't despair. Pictures for center backgrounds can be obtained from several sources:

A. Commercially prepared transparencies may be projected on a sheet of oaktag. Trace around the image with a marking pen, and color in the areas with other marking pens, crayons, or paint.

B. Prepare your own transparencies by running a favorite picture through a thermofax machine. Then follow the procedure above.

C. Trace a favorite picture on a sheet of clear acetate. Use an overhead projector and follow the same procedure above.

D. Project a favority picture onto a sheet of oaktag using an opaque projector.

E. Cut out favorite illustrations from magazines and newspapers, store displays, advertising circulars, coloring books, etc. Paste the pictures on heavy tagboard to create your center background.

*7. Create centers in a variety of shapes and place them in different spots in the classroom.*

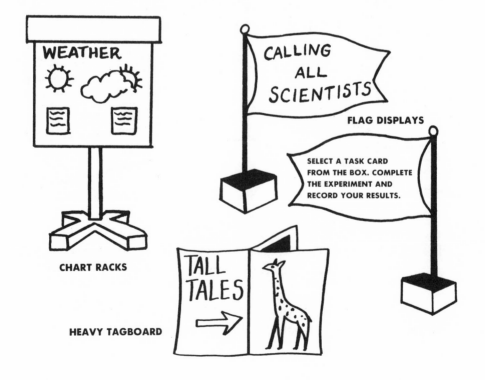

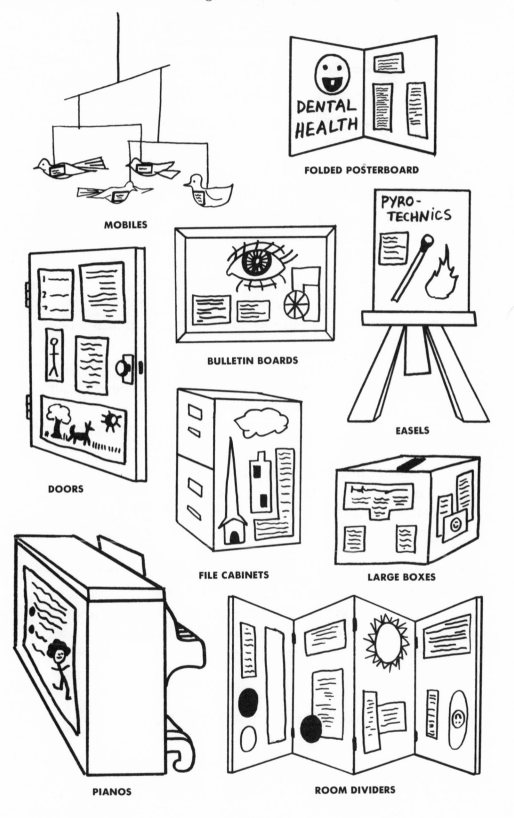

MOBILES

FOLDED POSTERBOARD

DENTAL HEALTH

DOORS

BULLETIN BOARDS

PYRO-TECHNICS

EASELS

FILE CABINETS

LARGE BOXES

PIANOS

ROOM DIVIDERS

## Sample Step-By-Step Procedure in Creating a Learning Center

1. Choose an area of your curriculum in which you would like to begin. Most teachers feel comfortable starting with either reading or math.

| |
|---|
| *Example:*    Math |

2. Determine the purpose for your learning center. Most teachers prefer to begin with centers geared to the reinforcement of skills already introduced through group instruction.

| |
|---|
| *Example:*    To reinforce simple basic addition and subtraction skills. |

3. Select learning activities that interest children; that can be done independently; and that meet the purpose(s) which you have identified. Teachers generally find that manipulative activities and games are popular choices with children.

| |
|---|
| *Example:*    My children will reinforce their skills in addition and subtraction by participating in these simple independent activities: |

### ACTIVITY A. CLOTHESPIN GAME

The children must use the appropriate clothespin to hang the clothes on the line.

## ACTIVITY B. TWO-WAY RACE

| | 7 | 8 | 3 | 6 | 5 | 1 | 9 | 6 | 2 | 10 | |
|---|---|---|---|---|---|---|---|---|---|---|---|
| | +3 | +4 | +2 | +5 | +5 | +6 | +8 | +6 | +7 | +9 | |

Write computation problems on a sheet of heavy tagboard. Laminate the board so that it can be erased after each game is completed. Two children play, each beginning at opposite ends of the board. At a given signal (called by another child, an aide, the teacher), the children start writing answers to each of the problems on the laminated board. They work toward each other until they meet. At that point, the child with the greater number of correct answers is the winner.

## ACTIVITY C. COMPUTER GAME

2 + 5 = 7

Students must flip the cards on the stand to create a correct math sentence.

## ACTIVITY D.  BEAN BAG MATH

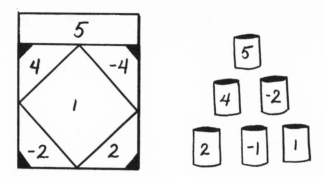

Create a board, or use large juice cans, which can be placed on the floor. The children take turns, each one tossing three bean bags onto the board or into the cans. They total their score for each round, and add scores for successive rounds. First player to reach 25 points wins the game.

4.  Provide means for self-correction for the activities in your learning center.

*Example:*

Activity A.  Correct answers are on the reverse side of the articles of clothing, under flaps if you wish.

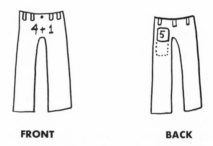

Activity B.  Correct answers are on the reverse side of the game board.

| | | 10 | 12 | 5 | 1 | 10 | 7 | 17 | 12 | 9 | 19 | |
|---|---|---|---|---|---|---|---|---|---|---|---|---|

BACK

Activity C and Activity D.  A center director (the teacher, an aide, or a student whose math skills are beyond the work of these centers) will be on hand to check the answers.

5. Construct clear direction cards for each activity.

*Example:*

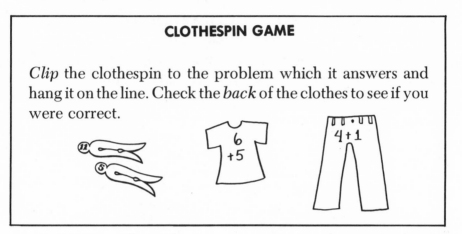

**CLOTHESPIN GAME**

*Clip* the clothespin to the problem which it answers and hang it on the line. Check the *back* of the clothes to see if you were correct.

6. Mount the activities on an attractive background which will draw the children to the learning center.

*Example:*

I usually fasten the direction cards to the center background with brass fasteners. This makes it easy to change center activities in any way desired. Gluing or pasting direction cards to the center background causes great difficulty when removing or replacing activities.

7. Introduce the children to their new classroom experience. A careful introduction is needed if the children have had little or no previous experience in the use of learning centers. Show the children what the center contains and how it is to be used. The direction cards will reinforce your verbal directions.

TURN TO THE NEXT SECTION FOR MANY
CREATIVE LEARNING CENTER IDEAS!

# SECTION II

# IDEAS AND ACTIVITIES:
## Models from Which to Choose

Each learning center idea presented here consists of several activities. Teachers are urged to use the learning centers in ways that would be appropriate for their particular groups of children—the centers may be used as is, with all component activities; only some activities may be selected for use; other activities may be added; or desired activities or formats may be adapted for use at other grade levels or for other subject areas.

The following format has been used to present each learning center: The first page introduces and explains the learning center as a whole. The picture represents the bulletin board the teacher might create for displaying the theme of the center to the children. On this bulletin board, the teacher may attach the directions for each of the component activities that comprise the center.

Next, each activity contained in that center is described in detail. There are directions to the teacher for making the project, and directions for how the children are to use it. Sample stories, worksheets, materials have been included where needed.

LEARNING CENTER NO. 1                    Level: KINDERGARTEN

## Can You Tell the Difference?

Curriculum Area:  READING READINESS, VISUAL AND TACTILE
                  PERCEPTION

Goal:  PROMOTING SKILLS

Even the youngest children can work independently in learning centers provided the activities are designed to be of interest to them and well within their abilities. At this center, children work at tasks which build needed skills and which they can complete successfully on their own.

In learning to read, children will ultimately need to bring to bear very fine visual perceptual abilities in distinguishing differences of shape, size, key features, direction, internal detail, in order to recognize letters and words. These skills will be gradually developed through many rich kindergarten experiences and activities. This center focuses on gross visual perception and general configuration as a first step in the path to reading. The activities are short and simple and well within the means of most children.

## GAMES AND ACTIVITIES

### 1. PHOTO MATCH

Take a front-view and back-view photograph of each child in your classroom. Mount the photos on oaktag to make them sturdy. Print the initials of the children on the backs. Mix up all of the photos and place them in a box. The children carefully examine the photos and match each front-view with its appropriate back-view. They are right if the initials match.

### 2. STICKER PUZZLES

Get a variety of gummed picture stickers in a variety or gift shop. Mount each sticker on a square of cardboard. Cut each square in half—vertically, horizontally, or diagonally. Mix up all of the cards and put them in a box. The children are to match the two halves which fit together to make a complete picture.

## 3. TEEPEE SHAPES

Cut a large, heavy sheet of posterboard into the shape of an Indian teepee. Cut out a variety of shapes from colored construction paper or tagboard. Make duplicates of each of these shapes. Paste one set on the teepee, and put a drapery hook through the top of each shape. Punch a hole in each of the second set of shapes. The children hang each shape on the teepee on the appropriate hook so that the shapes match.

## 4. MITTEN MATCH

Using wallpaper samples or gift wrap paper mounted on heavy tagboard, cut out many pairs of mittens, each pair with a different pattern. Put the mittens in a box and have the children match left and right mitten pairs.

## 5. PALM TRACE

Provide a paint brush and water soluble paint. Children work in pairs. One child shuts her eyes as the other child traces a number, letter, or geometric shape on her palm with the paint brush. The first child calls out the name of the letter, number, or shape, and then looks to see if she was right. The children switch roles.

LEARNING CENTER NO. 2                    Level: KG., GR. 1

## You'll Flip Over These Number Games

Curriculum Area:   MATH, NUMERATION

Goal:   PROMOTING SKILLS

This center provides manipulative activities that are of great interest to young children, and which give them experience and practice with numeration and with relating sets of objects to numerals in different contexts. The children recognize the numerals from one to ten and group the appropriate number of objects to go with each numeral.

The center is designed not only to reinforce math skills, but to provide children, at very early ages, with activities that they can complete successfully by themselves or with a partner. They learn good habits and procedures for working independently.

## GAMES AND ACTIVITIES

### 1. MARBLES AND JARS

Collect ten small baby food jars and label them with the numerals one through ten. Provide a box with lots of marbles. Two children work together. One child examines the numeral printed on each jar, drops in the appropriate number of marbles, and screws the jar lid back on. The child then gets a classmate to open each jar and count the marbles to check if the correct amount was put there. The marbles then go back into the box.

## 2. JUNK BOX COUNT

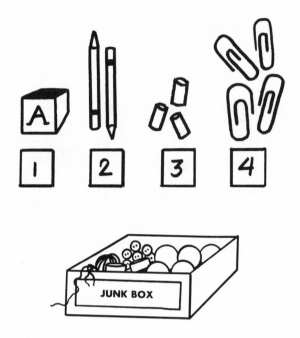

Collect a different number of various familiar objects, such as: one building block, two pencils, three rubber erasers, four paper clips, five rubber bands, etc. Place all of the objects in a large box, labeled "Junk Box." Prepare 3″ x 3″ tagboard cards, each with a numeral from one to ten on it.

The children take the objects out of the Junk Box and group identical objects in sets. They then take a tagboard numeral and place it under the set it corresponds with.

The teacher or center director should be available to check the child's work once the activity has been completed. Ask questions such as: "How many rubber bands did you count?" "Do you have more rubber bands or more paper clips?" "Are there less pencils or less blocks?"

## 3. MARBLE DROP

Provide ten paper cups, each labeled with a numeral from one to ten. Put the corresponding number of marbles in each cup. Also, provide a metal pie tin or tin can.

Two students play this game. One child turns her back on the second child. The second child randomly selects a cup, takes the marbles out, and slowly drops the marbles into the pan one at a time so that they can be heard easily. The first child (with back turned) listens carefully, counting to herself the number of marbles which were dropped. She then identifies which cup the marbles were from. The marbles then go back into the cup. The children take turns dropping the marbles and guessing.

## 4. PLANT A NUMERAL

metal washer

Using construction paper, make ten flower pots containing only the stems and bottom leaves of plants. On each pot, draw a number of dots ranging from one to ten. Glue a metal washer to the top of each flower stem. Mount the pots on a strip of heavy tagboard and fasten to or hang on the wall. Make ten flower blossoms out of construction paper. In the center of each flower, put a numeral from one to ten. Glue a small magnet to the back of each flower. Put the flowers in a box.

The child places each flower on the washer of the plant it goes with. The teacher or learning center director should be available to check the child's work.

## 5. LACING NUMBERS

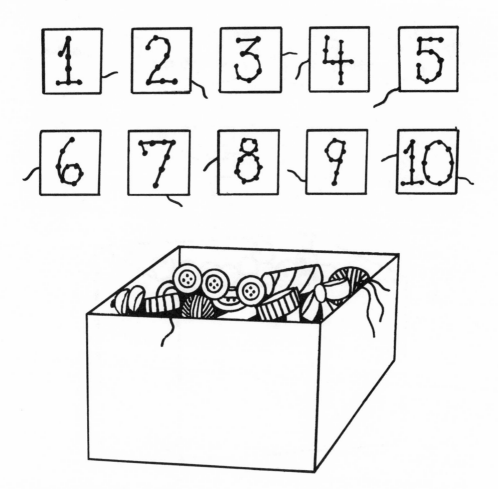

Cut many seven-inch squares out of tagboard. Lightly draw a large numeral ranging from one to ten on each square. Make many such sets of cards. Punch holes at even intervals along the numeral. (Erase the pencil marks that are left on the numeral.) Provide large needles and colorful yarn for the children. The children are to lace in and out of the holes until the numeral design appears.

Provide a box or can filled with small counters (buttons, chips, elbow noodles). When the child finishes sewing, she takes a set of objects equivalent to the numeral on the card and pastes them to the card. Children may take their cards home.

## 6. NUMBER NECKLACE

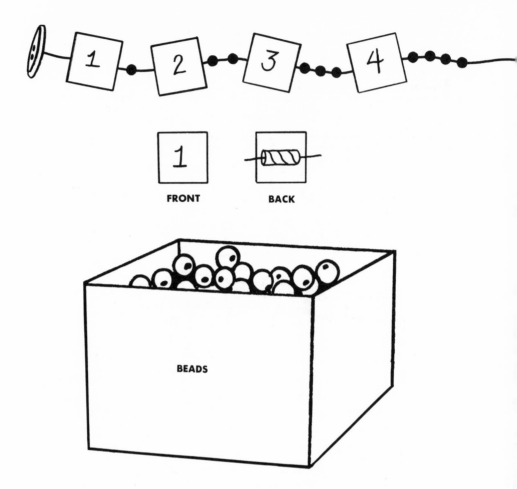

FRONT          BACK

BEADS

Cut long pieces of string or yarn, and tie a button at one end of each piece. Make sets of tagboard squares with numerals from one to ten. Cut drinking straws into half-inch pieces. Glue a section of drinking straw to the back of each numeral square (for stringing). Put many wooden beads in a box.

The children string the number *one* card on the yarn, followed by one bead. The number *two* card is strung next, followed by two beads. The children continue in this way, stringing each numeral in sequence, followed by the appropriate number of beads. When they finish (having strung ten beads at the end), help them make a loop at the end of the yarn to hook over the button. They may take their necklaces home.

LEARNING CENTER NO. 3                    Level: KG., GR. 1

# The Letter Chef

Curriculum Area:  LANGUAGE ARTS, ALPHABETICAL ORDER,
                  LETTER RECOGNITION
      Goal:  PROMOTING SKILLS

One of the reading readiness skills involves familiarity with the alphabet, knowing the sequence of the letters, and recognizing the printed forms of the letters, both in upper and lower case. These skills depend on visual perception and memory, and they need lots of practice. At this center, play activities that are enjoyable in and of themselves give the young child opportunities for practicing these skills. At the same time, the child is learning habits of working independently.

## GAMES AND ACTIVITIES

## 1. FEEL THE LETTER

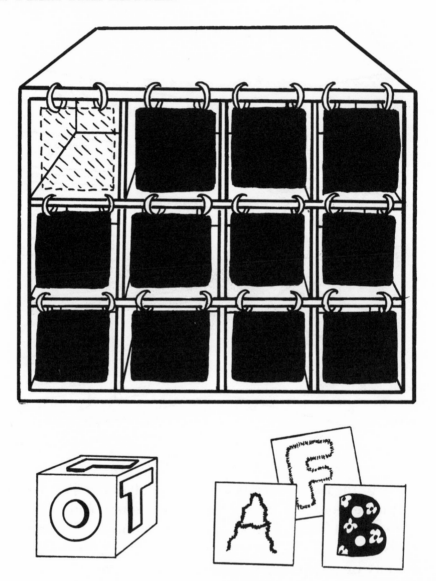

Get a carton that has partitions in it (like the carton a liquor store uses for a case of wine). Stand it on its side, with the open partitions facing you.

Attach a piece of fabric to the top of each section of the

carton, so that the fabric covers the open front of the section. On separate index cards, paste letters made out of various materials, i.e., "A" from sandpaper, "B" from pipecleaners, "C" from aluminum foil, etc. Put one card on the bottom of each section of the carton. Have some alphabet blocks at the learning center.

The children place their hands into one of the sections, and try to determine with their sense of touch which letter of the alphabet is on the card. They then find that letter on the block and check their work by removing the card and looking at it to see if it matches the letter on the block.

Put new cards, with different letters, in the box every week or so.

## 2. LETTER BAGS

| LETTER BAGS WORKSHEET | | | | | LETTER BAGS ANSWER SHEET |
|---|---|---|---|---|---|
| BAG NO. 1 | A | C | D | F | BAG NO. 1—C |
| BAG NO. 2 | B | D | E | G | BAG NO. 2—B |
| BAG NO. 3 | I | K | M | O | BAG NO. 3—M |
| BAG NO. 4 | Q | S | U | X | BAG NO. 4—U |
| BAG NO. 5 | Z | B | C | E | BAG NO. 5—Z |
| BAG NO. 6 | F | H | J | L | BAG NO. 6—L |
| BAG NO. 7 | N | P | R | T | BAG NO. 7—P |
| BAG NO. 8 | V | X | Y | C | BAG NO. 8—C |

Prepare eight drawstring bags and number them one through eight. Make or buy plastic or cardboard letters. Place one letter in each bag. Prepare worksheets as in the sample, and provide an answer key.

The child places her hand into one of the bags and attempts to identify the letter by touch. She then takes a dittoed worksheet and circles the letter which she believes to be in the bag. When all bags are done, she checks her work with the answer key.

## 3. BALLOON STAND

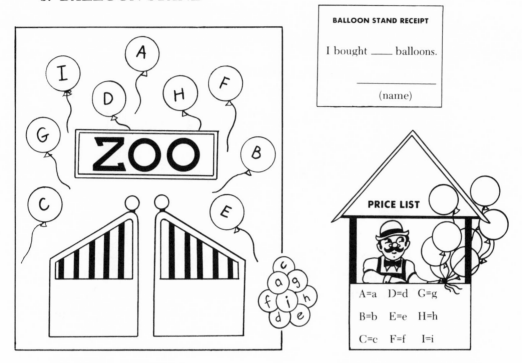

BALLOON STAND RECEIPT

I bought _____ balloons.

_____

(name)

PRICE LIST

A=a   D=d   G=g

B=b   E=e   H=h

C=c   F=f   I=i

Using construction paper, cut out colorful balloons and fasten them to a large oaktag game board. Print one upper case letter on each balloon. Cut out additional circles from construction paper, and print the corresponding lower case letters on these circles. Mix them up and put them in a folder.

Make up an answer sheet in the form of a "Price List for a Balloon Stand" (as in the illustrated example). Put this in a folder, and mark the folder, "Check Your Work." Ditto copies of a "Balloon Stand Receipt" and include these in the folder.

The children match the circles with the lower case letters by placing them on the balloons with the appropriate upper case letters. They check their own work by looking at the Price List in the folder. They also record the number of letters correctly matched by completing the receipt form.

To make for easy progression from easy to more difficult, you might start by using for your game board the letters that remain largely the same in lower and upper case form (c, o, k, s, v, w, x, y, z). When the children can successfully complete this work independently, the game board can be changed to include letters whose capitals differ from the lower case forms.

## 4. ALPHABET STREET

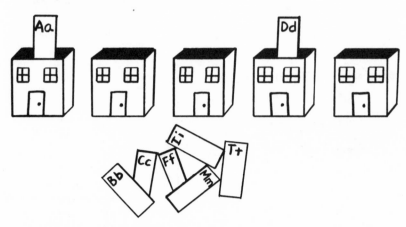

Cut the tops off twenty-six pint milk cartons. Cover each carton with colored paper and draw windows and a door on each. Print one letter of the alphabet on the back of each house. Line up the houses in alphabetical order to form a street. Prepare twenty-six cards, printing one letter of the alphabet in upper and lower case at the top. Make the cards tall enough so that when they are placed into the milk cartons, the letters may be seen on top of the houses.

Two children play this game. One child sits in back of the houses, and one child in front. The child in back places the letter cards into the houses in proper alphabetical order. She can tell the correct order by matching the letters on the cards with the letters on the backs of the houses. She places the cards so that the letters are facing the front of the house and her classmate can see them. When they are all in alphabetical order, the child in back removes several of the cards from the houses, shuffles them, and hands them to the child in front. This child attempts to place the shuffled cards back into the houses so that the proper alphabetical order is maintained. The child in the back sees if the order is correct. They do this several times, and then they change places and repeat the activity.

Provide paper so that the children may copy the alphabet when they are finished playing.

## 5. ICE CREAM CONES

Cut twenty-six cones out of construction paper. Write the alphabet, using capital letters, on the cones. Put the cones in an envelope. Cut out twenty-six pieces of construction paper, each one in the shape of a scoop of ice cream, and write the alphabet, using lower case letters, on these. Put them in another envelope.

The children are to arrange the cones in alphabetical order on a table or the floor. They are then to put a scoop of ice cream on each cone, matching the lower case letter with the capital letter.

If you have the alphabet displayed somewhere in your room, the children can check their work with this. If not, provide an answer key in a folder.

LEARNING CENTER NO. 4                                    Level: GR. 1, 2

# Community Helpers

Curriculum Area:   SOCIAL STUDIES, COMMUNITY WORKERS
Goal:   CONCEPT DEVELOPMENT

This center provides follow-up activities to supplement and reinforce concepts about community helpers developed through direct experience on field trips, or through books and other materials. At this center, children demonstrate their knowledge of what the various community helpers do, and what special tools they use to perform their jobs.

## GAMES AND ACTIVITIES

## 1. JOB TOOLS

DOCTOR          TEACHER          POLICEWOMAN          FIREMAN

REPAIRMAN          CHEF          MAILMAN

Draw or find pictures of community workers in old work-books or coloring books. Mount them on a large posterboard hung over a table. Label each picture. Beneath each picture, on the table, place a pie tin. Place a large box on the table. In it, put small objects representing the equipment used by the workers pictured.

The activity for the children is to take the objects from the box and sort them into the appropriate pans, to show the tools associated with each community helper.

## 2. WHO AM I?

I help you when
you are sick.

Using another set of pictures of community workers, paste the pictures on cardboard and color them. Cut out each figure. Now create a set of silhouettes by tracing around each figure and cutting around the outlined forms. Write a clue for each worker. For example: "I help you when you are sick." "I bring you letters." "I fix things when they break." Place the colored figures in one box, the silhouetted figures in another box, and the clues in a third box.

The children are to use each clue to identify the worker it describes, and match the colored picture with its silhouette.

A letter, symbol, or number code may be placed on the back of each picture and each clue card, so that the children can check their own work when they have finished.

## 3. HELP ME!

Prepare a set of "Help Me!" cards for each community worker. Each set should illustrate the sequence of activities community workers follow in doing their jobs. About six pictures per community worker are appropriate. Pictures can be obtained by taking photographs on field trips, by cutting up old workbooks or coloring books, or by using the childrens' own drawings following a field trip.

Number or letter codes on the backs of the cards facilitate self-checking. Each set of cards may be put (in mixed-up order) in a separate envelope. The children are to arrange the pictures to show the order in which a community helper does his job.

## 4. MY OWN MOVIE

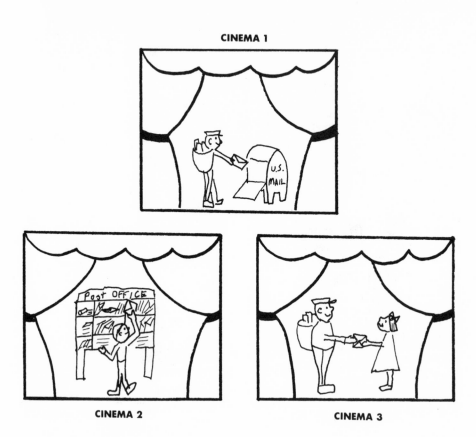

Prepare duplicated papers (as in the example) which provide a beginning to a story involving a community helper. The story starter can be written or drawn, depending on the ability level of your children. Encourage the students to finish the story by drawing or writing on the movie screens the next two or three important things that happened in the order that they happened. *Example:*

> Joey was happy because it was his best friend's birthday. Joey bought a very nice birthday card for his friend. Joey signed the card. Then he wrote his friend's name and address on the envelope, placed a stamp on it, and took the card to the mailbox on the corner. WHAT HAPPENED NEXT?

LEARNING CENTER NO. 5                    Level: GR. 1, 2

## The Addition-Subtraction Pond

Curriculum Area:  MATH, ADDITION AND SUBTRACTION

Goal:  PROMOTING SKILLS

This is a reinforcement center for skills taught in previous lessons. When they are first learning mathematical facts, young children need a great deal of practice to wean them away from finger-counting, and to help them make addition and subtraction computations quickly and automatically. Games are an excellent means for providing such drill, because motivation is high. The games should be easy enough and yet challenging enough so that the children have both the interest and the skills to win.

## GAMES AND ACTIVITIES

### 1. SNAIL TRAIL

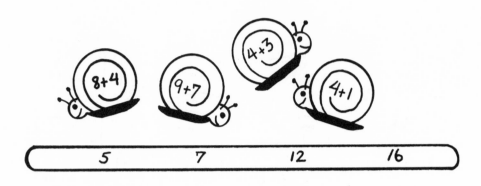

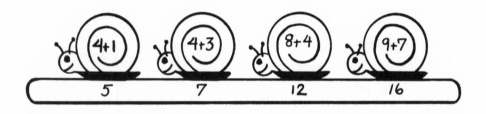

Using tagboard or heavy construction paper, make a number of snails and label each with an addition or subtraction computation problem. You may put the answers on the backs of the snails, under flaps if you wish, for self-checking. Now make a number of snail trails, randomly placing the answers to the snail problems along the trails.

The child puts a snail trail on the floor or table, finds the snails that match that trail, and places each snail at its appropriate location on the trail.

## 2. CATCH THE WORM

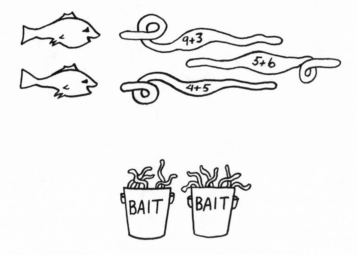

Cut out two fish, using heavy tagboard; laminate them so that they will be durable. Put them in an envelope. Cut out many worm shapes, using heavy tagboard. Write an addition or subtraction computation on each worm, and put the answer on the back. Laminate the worms, also, and put them in a box. Provide two bait cans.

Two children may play this game. They flip a coin to see who goes first. The first player randomly selects a worm from the box and places the worm next to her fish. If she can solve the computation problem on the worm, the worm goes into her bait can. If the problem is solved incorrectly, the child must leave the worm out on the table. The children continue in turn until there are no more worms in the box. The child who has the most worms in his bait can is the winner.

## 3. LADYBUG GAME BOARD

Cut out four large, colorful flowers and four green stems, and glue them to heavy tagboard. Glue ten small, metal washers, about two inches apart, along each flower stem and one to the center of the flower. Provide four magnetized ladybugs. Prepare a set of about fifty addition and subtraction computation problems on index cards.

Four children play. They take turns picking a computation problem from the deck of index cards. They check their answers on the backs of the cards. If the child gets the problem correct, he moves his magnetized ladybug ahead one washer. If he gives an incorrect answer, he stays where he is, places the card at the bottom of the pile, and waits for his next turn. The play continues until one child gets a ladybug to the center of the flower.

## 4. CATCH THE FLY

Using heavy tagboard or durable construction paper, cut out frogs, flies, and about fifteen to twenty lily pads. Write an addition or subtraction computation problem on each lily pad. Put the answers on the backs.

The child places the lily pads in a row on the floor or table. The frog is placed on the first lily pad and the fly on the fourth lily pad. The object of the game is to get the fly to the end of the row before it is captured by the frog.

The child answers the arithmetic problem on the fifth lily pad, and checks the answer on the back of the pad. If correct, the child moves the fly to that pad. The frog also moves ahead one lily pad. The child goes on to the problem on the next lily pad.

If, however, the child's answer was incorrect, she moves the frog one lily pad ahead but leaves the fly where it was.

The child goes on to try the problem on the next pad. The frog moves ahead one lily pad at every turn. Since the fly moves ahead one lily pad only when the child gives the correct answer, the frog will catch up with the fly if she misses three problems. This will indicate that more direct teaching is needed for this child.

## 5. MUSHROOM MATCH

Cut mushroom shapes out of construction paper and laminate them. Write an addition or subtraction computation on the top half, and the answer on the bottom half. Cut apart the tops of the mushrooms from the stems. Place all the problems in one box and all the answers in another box. The children are to match the tops and bottoms to make correct problem-answer combinations. They check the backs of the mushroom tops to see if their solutions are correct.

LEARNING CENTER NO. 6                    Level: GR., 1, 2

# Mother Goose on the Loose

Curriculum Area:  LANGUAGE ARTS, MOTHER GOOSE RHYMES
            Goal:  STIMULATING CREATIVITY

This center leads children to progress from passively reading and memorizing Mother Goose rhymes to actively interpreting, responding, and creating nonsense verse. The humor, fantasy, and symbols of Mother Goose are a traditional source of delight for young children. At this center, they get the opportunity to dramatize their favorite characters, and immortalize them in sensible and nonsensical writing tasks. They can then try their own hands at creating symbols and rhymes of their own.

## GAMES AND ACTIVITIES

### 1. MIXED-UP MOTHER GOOSE

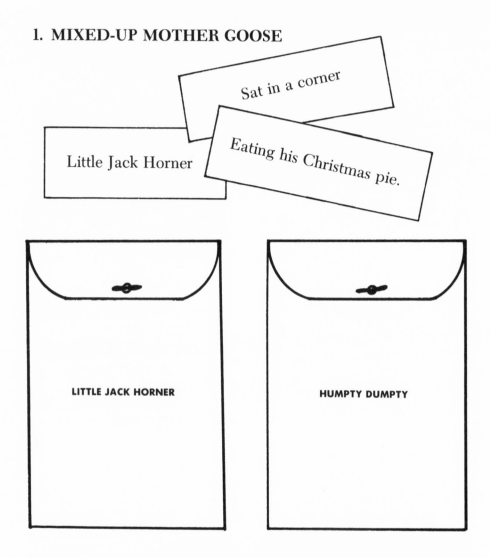

Print various Mother Goose rhymes on sheets of oaktag, and cut them into strips, line by line. Put all the strips (in mixed up order) for each rhyme in a separate envelope. Have a collection of Mother Goose books at the center. The children are to take the strips from each envelope and rearrange them in proper sequence. They check their own work by finding the rhyme in one of the books provided.

## 2. MOTHER GOOSE IN ACTION

For this activity, the children are to choose partners and work in pairs. They look through the Mother Goose books at the center and select a rhyme which they would like to pantomime. They practice in a corner or in the corridor, where no one can see them. Set aside a time of the day when each of the pairs can present their pantomime to the rest of the class. The others try to guess what rhyme the pantomimists are portraying.

## 3. MOTHER GOOSE HALL OF FAME

Make many plaques out of yellow construction paper. Make available sheets of writing paper. The children choose the Mother Goose rhyme they like best. Following the example and directions you have mounted, they draw a picture of the Mother Goose character they have selected on a plaque. On a separate sheet of paper, they write why they feel their character belongs in the Mother Goose Hall of Fame. Then they mount their plaque and story on the learning center background. Change the contributions as space dictates.

## 4. TELEGRAM

TELEGRAM

# WESTERN ～～ ONION

TO: *The Cow who jumped over the Moon*

FROM: *Jack*

*I don't believe the story about your jumping over the moon. I jumped over a very tall candlestick and I think I'm the best jumper in the world. I challenge you to a jumping contest at my place next Tuesday at 2:00. Be there!*

Provide a pad of blank telegrams. Instruct the children to try to imagine what might happen if some of the Mother Goose characters could communicate with each other. Each child is to pretend to be one Mother Goose character, writing a telegram to another Mother Goose character. They may ask for help (as in the cases of Humpty Dumpty or Jack and Jill) or just share feelings and ideas. Post a few samples of your own on the center background to stimulate the children's ideas. Post the children's work as they do it.

## 5. ADD A RHYME

In this activity, the children make up their own variations on Mother Goose verses. Make a colorful train engine, and place it where there is enough room for a long line of cars to follow (e.g., as a border over the blackboard). Start with just one rhyme. Behind the engine, mount one or two samples of variations on this traditional Mother Goose rhyme (e.g., "Hickory Dickory Dock" or "Old Mother Hubbard"). Provide additional blank construction-paper cars. Encourage children to change the traditional rhyme as you have done, to create an original verse. Add the children's verses to the growing train. When one Mother Goose rhyme has been exhausted, start again with another rhyme.

LEARNING CENTER NO. 7                          Level: GR., 1, 2

## Muncha Buncha Words

Curriculum Area:  READING, SIGHT VOCABULARY
        Goal:  PROMOTING SKILLS

Beginning reading instruction focuses upon several critical skills, among the most essential of which is the ability to develop a basic storehouse of sight words. The ability of children to recognize quickly and accurately an ever increasing fund of words will affect the ease with which they will later be able to comprehend sentences and longer passages. This center provides games and individual manipulative activities, designed to actively involve children in recognizing words appropriate to their reading levels.

This center may be adapted for any grade level whenever word recognition skills need strengthening.

## GAMES AND ACTIVITIES

## 1. YEA! BOO!

Cut off the tops of four small milk containers and paint or paper them. Label two boxes YEA! and two boxes BOO! Prepare a stack of words which the children have met in their reading. Place the word cards in a large coffee can.

Two players play this game. The children each take a YEA! box and a BOO! box. They take turns drawing cards from the word can. If the word is read correctly, it is placed in the child's YEA! box. If incorrectly read, it is placed in the child's BOO! box. The children check each other's work and consult the teacher in case of disagreement. When all the cards have been picked, the players count all their YEA! words and subtract from this number all the BOO! words. Higher score wins.

## 2. WORD CHECKERS

Draw a checkerboard on a large sheet of heavy tagboard. Print words in black on the squares on one half, and in red on the other half.

The children play checkers in the normal way, but they must be able to say the word before they can move or jump to that square. They check each other and consult the teacher in case of disagreement.

## 3. WORD JACKS

| BACK | FRONT | | BACK | FRONT |
|------|-------|---|------|-------|
| 1 | boy | | 2 | cane |
| 3 | fruit | | 4 | their |
| 5 | rough | | 6 | wrote |
| 7 | height | | 8 | cell |
| 9 | piece | | 10 | stranger |

Make available a set of jacks. Prepare stacks of word cards, number coding them from one to ten, for level of difficulty. The easiest words are numbered one, the most difficult, ten.

The children play jacks in the normal way, but before a player can pick up one jack, he must read a word card numbered one correctly. Before he can pick up two jacks, a number two word card must be read correctly, and so on. If the player makes a mistake, the card goes back in the pile and he tries another card with the same number on his next turn. The children continue in this way, until one child reads a word card labeled ten correctly, and picks up ten jacks.

## 4. "ZONK"

Prepare a deck of about thirty-five to forty sight word cards, plus four ZONK cards.

Two or more children may play this game. They check each other's work. The deck of cards is placed face down in the middle of the table. The players take turns drawing the top card from the deck. If the player can read the word, she may keep it. If she gets it wrong, the card goes on the bottom of the deck. If she gets a ZONK card, she may draw a second card. The ZONK card then goes on the bottom of the deck. The winner is the one who has the most cards when there are only ZONK cards left in the deck.

## 5. SPILL AND SORT

Cut the tops off three small milk cartons to make three sorting boxes. Label each with a different category. Write words associated with each category on tongue depressors. Put them in a box.

Two children may play this game. They spill out the tongue depressors, scattering them on the table top. They turn them face down, and then they take turns picking a word and sorting it into the correct box. If a player is wrong, he keeps the tongue depressor. When all the words have been sorted, the child who has fewer tongue depressors in hand wins. Both children copy the words they missed in their notebooks to study for the next time.

LEARNING CENTER NO. 8                          Level: GR., 1, 2

## Elephants Have Good Memories . . . Do You?

Curriculum Area:  READING, COMPREHENSION AND RECALL OF
                  SENTENCES AND PARAGRAPHS

        Goal:  PROMOTING SKILLS

   The beginning reader who is making the transition from word reading to idea reading needs lots of independent practice in simple comprehension skills. This center addresses itself to the reinforcement of comprehension at a simple, literal level. Through manipulative activities and interesting games, children are encouraged to read, understand, and remember sentences, paragraphs, and short stories, by translating written words into sequences of images and actions.

## GAMES AND ACTIVITIES

## 1. BRAIN TEASERS

Find pictures of busy scenes in magazines or old workbooks. Paste each picture on the top half of a large piece of tagboard. Create a flap at the bottom, as illustrated.

Print these directions on the front face of the flap:

Look at the picture for as long as you like. Then turn the flap over so that it covers the picture.

Answer the questions without looking back at the picture.

Write your answers on a paper and then get the answer key and check your work.

Look at the picture again to see what mistakes you made.

Write about ten yes-no questions on the inside of the flap, such as:

1. There were four people in the picture.

2. It was nighttime.

3. The dog was brown.

4. It was winter.

5. A boy was running.

6. There were two cars and a bus in the picture.

7. A woman was carrying a baby.

8. The dog was running after the boy.

9. A woman was wearing a red coat.

10. Nobody was wearing a hat.

Adapt the pictures and questions to the appropriate reading level for your children. For beginning readers, they will be simple, concrete sentences. At later stages, they can be more complex and more abstract, and the forms of the questions can vary as well.

Provide an answer key.

## 2. MYSTERY BOX

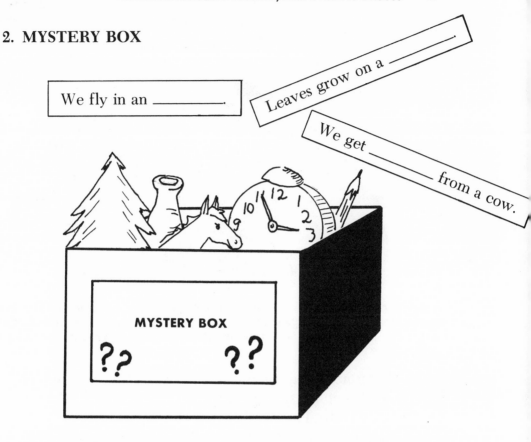

On strips of construction paper (about 4″ x 15″), write sentences leaving one word blank. On the back of the strip, write the word that goes in the blank. Supply a "Mystery Box" with objects which could be placed on the cards to complete the sentences.

The child places all the sentence strips on the table or floor, reaches into the Mystery Box, picks out an object, and places it on the proper sentence card. When all the sentences are complete, the child takes a piece of paper and writes the names of the objects used to complete each sentence. Checking one sentence at a time by looking at the back of the sentence strip, the child puts each object back into the box.

## 3. PICTURE CAPTIONS

BOXER CHEWED UP
JIMMY'S FATHER'S SLIPPER.

JIMMY'S FATHER WAS
ANGRY. HE SAID THE PUPPY
HAD TO BE PUNISHED.

JIMMY HAD TO PUT
BOXER IN THE DOG HOUSE.
THEY WERE BOTH VERY SAD.

Look through magazines, old workbooks, travel folders, etc., and collect pictures that tell a story in sequence (or draw the pictures yourself). Paste the pictures on heavy tagboard. Write a short paragraph about each picture on additional pieces of tagboard. Put number or letter codes on the backs of the pictures and paragraphs for self-checking. Put each picture-story sequence in a separate envelope or folder.

The children are to match the paragraphs to the pictures and arrange them in sequence. When they finish one story and check their work, they may go to the next picture-story sequence. If the children work in pairs at this activity, they can dramatize each story when they finish it.

## 4. ELEPHANT-TOE

Using heavy tagboard, make a nine-inch square tic-tac-toe card and a set of three-inch square tic-tac-toe markers. Write two or three short elephant stories (like the sample here), and place each one in a story folder. Prepare a worksheet with nine questions for each story. Write each answer on a separate strip of paper; fold and number the answer strips. Place the questions and answers in folders.

The two children who are playing read the story. Then they take turns answering the questions and checking to see if they are right. When a child answers correctly, she places her marker on her tic-tac-toe board. The first child to get a straight line in any direction is the winner.

*Sample story:*

> Bomba, the elephant, was walking in the forest. He heard a funny noise. He looked behind the tree.

There he saw a baby gazelle crying. "What's wrong?" Bomba asked.

"I was walking with my family and then I ran off to follow a monkey. The monkey climbed a tree. And now I'm lost."

"Do not worry. I will help you find your family," said Bomba. "Follow me."

So Bomba led the gazelle back to his family. Everyone was so happy to see Gerry again. They gave Bomba lots of hay and peanuts.

*Sample questions:*

1. What was the elephant's name?

2. What was the gazelle's name?

3. What noise did the elephant hear?

4. Why was the gazelle crying?

5. How did the gazelle get lost?

6. Where did the monkey go?

7. How did the gazelle get back home?

8. Was the gazelle's family angry with him?

9. How did the gazelle's family thank the elephant?

## 5. STORY SPOTLIGHT

Have a supply of simple story books (basal readers, library books, Scholastic books) available. Provide drawing paper, crayons, marking pens, etc. The children choose a story to read, and then they draw pictures illustrating the sequence of events in the story.

Later, in a group sharing period, allow each child to explain the story. After turning off all the lights in the room, have the children tack their pictures up on the wall, and light up each panel with a flashlight as they tell the story in sequence.

LEARNING CENTER NO. 9                                    Level: GR. 2

# Number Fun

Curriculum Area:  MATH, ADDITION
            Goal:  PROMOTING SKILLS

Memorizing basic mathematics facts is frequently looked upon as a most boring learning experience by a great majority of children. At this center, addition and subtraction facts become learned and reinforced in a much more enjoyable way than with the usual drill. Learning basic facts becomes fun as children compete individually or with their friends in games and manipulative activities that require them to use addition and subtraction of sums below twenty.

**GAMES AND ACTIVITIES**

## 1. ADDITION RACETRACK

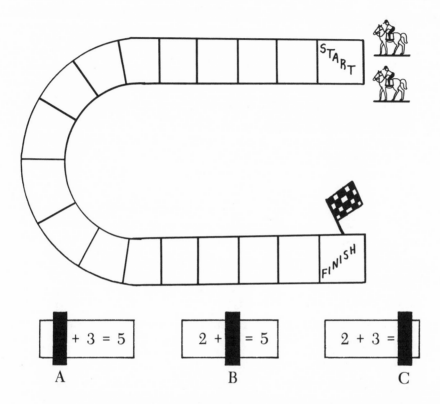

Make a horse race game board as shown. Small plastic toy horses can be used as markers. Make flash cards out of tagboard with addition facts. Cut out a strip of construction paper wide enough to cover a numeral and long enough to fit snugly around the flash card. Paste the ends of the strip together, and encircle each flash card with a construction paper strip, making sure it can slide back and forth easily.

Two children play together. They divide the flash cards between them. The players take turns. One picks a flash card and shows it to the other player, with the construction strip in position A, B, or C. The opponent must tell what numeral is covered by the strip. If correct, the player may move her horse one space forward. If incorrect, the horse must stay where it is. The first player to the finish line is the winner.

## 2. NUMBER LINE

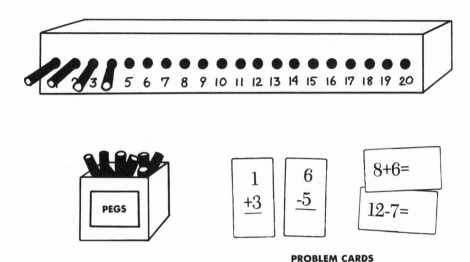

PROBLEM CARDS

Make a number line out of a wooden 2″ x 4″ block about twenty inches long. Drill twenty holes into the block and print the numerals from one to twenty beneath the holes. Make a set of cards with addition problems whose sums range from one to twenty, and with simple subtraction problems. Provide a box full of wooden pegs.

The children take turns drawing problem cards. The child reads the problem and calls out the answer. Then he works out the answer by putting pegs into the block. If the answer was correct, he keeps the card. If not, it goes back into the deck. The player who has kept the most cards wins the game.

## 3. PEBBLE TOSS

**PEBBLE TOSS WORKSHEET**

Name _____

Date _____

___ + ___ = ___

___ + ___ = ___

___ + ___ = ___

___ + ___ = ___

___ + ___ = ___

___ + ___ = ___

Divide the bottom of a shoe box into ten sections. Print a numeral from one to ten in each section. Put two pebbles in the box, and stretch a cover of clear plastic across the top. Provide worksheets for the children to write on.

The children shake the box and then put it down on a table. They add together the two numbers on which the pebbles landed, and record their work on the worksheet. After completing ten such problems, they put their worksheets in a basket for the teacher to check. Just for fun, the teacher may add up each child's total rolls to see who rolled the highest total score.

## 4. AUTO RACE

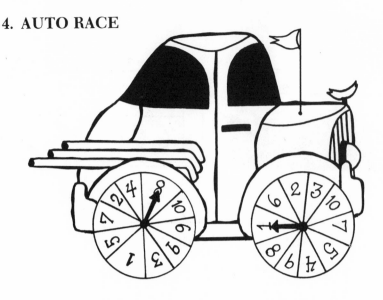

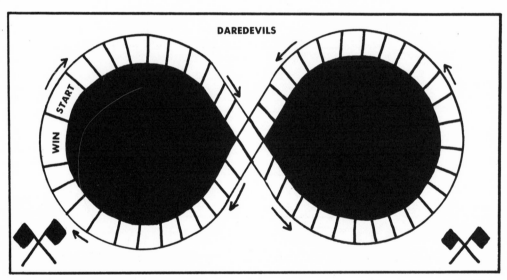

Draw the outline of a car on heavy tagboard. Make two spinners for the wheels, writing the numerals from one to ten on the sections of each spinner. Make a game board as illustrated, and provide toy cars for the children to use as markers.

The children take turns spinning both wheels. They add the two numerals shown and check each other's answers, consulting the teacher in case of disagreement. Each time a child gets the problem correct, he moves ahead one space. The first player to reach the finish line is the winner.

## 5. GO FISH

Make a deck of about fifty-two cards. Write the numerals from one to twenty on twenty cards. Write an addition problem whose sum is between one and twenty on each of the remaining cards.

The dealer shuffles the cards and deals seven to each player. The rest of the cards are placed in a pile face down. Before play starts, the players examine their cards. If they have any pairs of matched cards (e.g. 5 + 4 and 9 ; or 6 + 5 and 11 ; or 3 + 4 and 2 + 5 ; etc.), they place them face up in front of them.

The dealer starts the play. She asks any one of the other players for a card with a numeral that will match one in her hand. For example, if she has a 9 in her hand, she may ask another player, "Mike, do you have a card with 5 and 4?" If Mike has it, he must give it up. The dealer then shows her pair and places it in front of her. If Mike doesn't have that card, he tells the dealer to "Go Fish." The dealer takes a card from the pile of extra cards. Play continues in the same manner until the "fish" deck is gone. The player with the most pairs is the winner.

LEARNING CENTER NO. 10                    Level: GR. 2 AND UP

# Go Places With . . . Spelling

Curriculum Area: LANGUAGE ARTS, SPELLING

Goal: PROMOTING SKILLS

Spelling is often the bane of a child's existence and the bone of contention for adults. Spelling correctly requires visual and auditory perception and just plain practice and memorization. But children, like adults, tend to forget things that are boring. This center provides children with fascinating activities that they can engage in alone or with a partner, that will sharpen their spelling power by embedding spelling words in an interesting, vivid context. The center may be adapted to all grade levels simply by using appropriate words in the various formats.

## GAMES AND ACTIVITIES

## 1. WORD CARDS

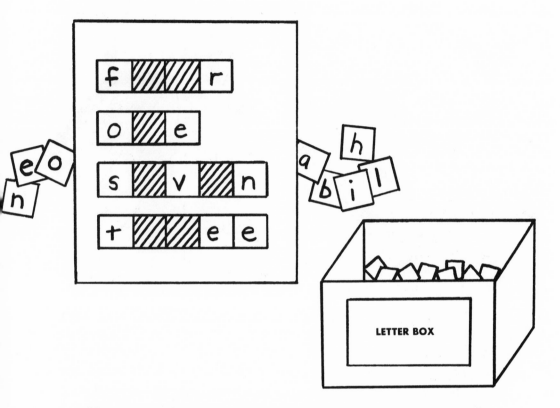

Choose words with which the class needs spelling practice. Cut white drawing paper into one and a half inch strips and block off the appropriate number of one and a half inch squares to accomodate a spelling word on each strip. (Each block will represent one letter of that word.) Glue or tape the strips to sheets of colored construction paper—about six strips per sheet. Fill in some of the letters of each spelling word to serve as clues. For younger classes, an identifying picture may accompany each word strip. Make many separate one and a half inch squares, and write all the needed letters on them. Put them in a box. Prepare an answer sheet and put it in a folder or an envelope.

The children examine the strips and fill in the missing letters, picking those letters out of the letter box. They check their own work with the answer sheet.

## 2. ROLLIN' ALONG

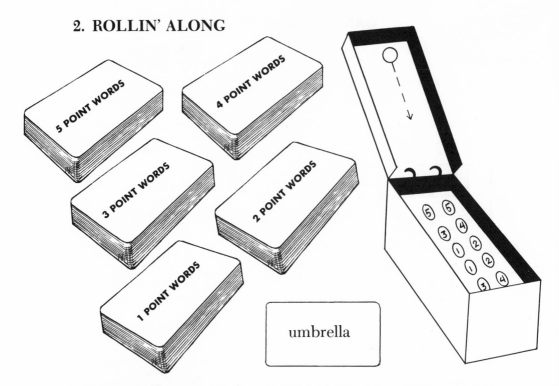

Using different colored construction paper, prepare five sets of word cards. Print all the easiest spelling words on one color and label this deck 1 POINT WORDS. The hardest spelling words will go in the 5 POINT WORDS deck. (For young children, in addition, draw or paste a picture on the card to illustrate the printed word.)

Now prepare a game as follows: Cut one of the short ends off a shoe box lid, and attach it to the shoe box using two strings which serve as hinges. Make the string taut enough so that the lid slants into the box. Glue the bottom of an egg carton to the bottom of the shoe box. Write the numbers one through five in the compartments of the egg carton.

Two or more children play this game. They take turns placing a small ping pong or rubber ball at the top of the lid and letting it roll down into an egg compartment. They choose any card from the deck with the number they rolled and without looking at the card, hand it to one of the other players. That player says the spelling word out loud for the child who just rolled to spell. If the word is spelled correctly, the child gets the points. The first player to reach thirty points is the winner.

## 3. SPELLING FORTUNE TELLERS

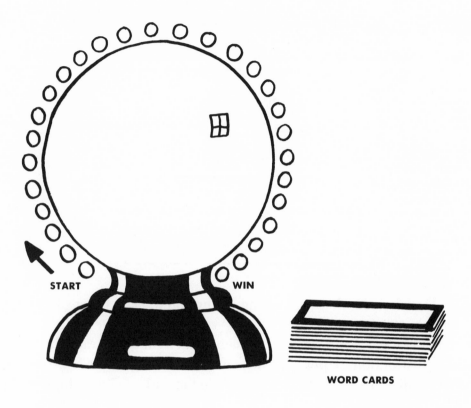

WORD CARDS

Make a game board by drawing a large crystal ball on cardboard, as in the illustration. Prepare a deck of cards using the week's word list. On each card, print a word, and also write a phrase or sentence to define or describe the word, for example, "JACKET—a short coat." The cards may be changed every week, or as often as necessary.

Both players place their markers at the starting point. They take turns, with one child picking a card and reading the defining clue to the other child, who tries to guess the word. If she guesses and spells it correctly, she moves her marker ahead one space. The first player to go around the crystal ball wins.

## 4. SPY MISSION

THIS 7/1/13/5

IS GREAT 6/20/14

TO 16/12/1/25

WITH A

6/18/9/5/14/4!

---

**CODE KEY**

A = 1, B = 2. . . . . . . . . . Z = 26

---

Develop a code by assigning a numeral to each letter of the alphabet, for example, A=26, B=25 . . . Z=1. Include the code key at the center. Write several messages, each on a separate sheet of construction paper. Include in the message words from the spelling list, writing those words in the code you developed. For example, "The 25/15/6/22 sky was a welcome 9/22/15/18/22/21 after 22/18/20/19/7 days of 24/15/12/6/23/8."

Have the children figure out the coded words. Provide an answer key with which they can check their work. Then have them use the code to create their own messages for others to decipher. Add these to the center after you check them out.

## 5. TRY AND FIND US

**TRY AND FIND US!**

| O | O | E | F | I | N | K |
|---|---|---|---|---|---|---|
| L | W | B | O | U | Y | R |
| E | Q | L | U | N | G | E |
| B | T | N | R | O | R | A |
| A | Z | O | I | A | R | D |
| L | V | R | G | K | P | Y |

**FIND SEVEN SPELLING WORDS.**

**LOOK ACROSS, DOWN, UP, DIAGONALLY.**

Create a maze of letters in which current spelling words are hidden. For younger children, have the words read horizontally only. For older children, the words may read in any and every direction—diagonally, up, down, from left to right, or from right to left.

The children find the hidden words and write them on a separate sheet of paper. They then check their work with the answer key.

LEARNING CENTER NO. 11                              Level: GR. 2, 3

# Money Matters

Curriculum Area:  MATH, MONEY

Goal:  PROMOTING SKILLS

There seems to be no better way of learning about money than by working directly with it. This center is designed for just that purpose. Children are encouraged to practice the use of money in several different realistic contexts. Experience is gained as children shop for food, buy lunch for a friend, play on a money game board, and even participate in a money contest. Children learn to work with one another while promoting their math concepts. They learn the value of each coin, the equivalencies of various combinations of coins, and how to combine various coins to produce specific money sums.

## GAMES AND ACTIVITIES

## 1. THE SHOPPING TRIP

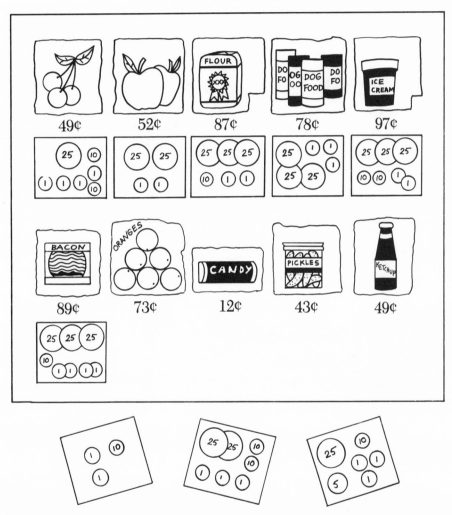

Cut out advertisements from the food section of a newspaper or advertising circular. Include prices for each item. Mount them on large 24" x 36" sheets of oaktag. Prepare small oaktag cards and on each card paste pictures of coins, showing the exact price of each of the food items. Write the total price on the back of each card. The children match the money cards to the food items, and check their answers by seeing if the price on the back of the card matches the price on the item they matched it to.

## 2. TAKE A FRIEND TO LUNCH

### LUNCH MENU

| | |
|---|---|
| Hamburger | 40¢ |
| French Fries | 15¢ |
| Hot Dog | 25¢ |
| Tuna Sandwich | 35¢ |
| Fried Chicken | 50¢ |
| Cola | 15¢ |
| Ice Cream | 10¢ |
| Cake | 15¢ |

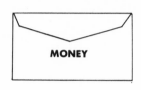

MONEY

| | | | | |
|---|---|---|---|---|
| Hamburger | 25¢ | 10¢ | 5¢ | 40¢ |
| French Fries | 10¢ | 5¢ | | 15¢ |
| Cola | 10¢ | 5¢ | | 15¢ |
| Ice Cream | 10¢ | | | 10¢ |
| Cake | 10¢ | 5¢ | | 15¢ |
| Billy | (25¢) (25¢) (25¢) (10¢) (10¢) | | | 95¢ |

Prepare a lunch menu, listing some favorite lunch foods and their prices. Provide a quantity of money stamps or paper coins in an envelope.

The children each choose a friend to take to lunch. Each child picks out a meal for the other child and writes the names of the food items and their prices on a piece of paper. They add up the prices and record the total cost. They then exchange lists. Each child pastes the coins they could use to pay for the lunch on the paper. They check each other's work.

## 3. MONEY BANKS

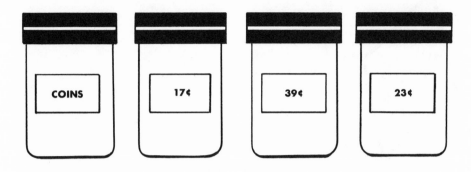

Make slits in the covers of baby food jars so they can serve as banks. Mark each jar with a different amount of money. Provide one jar with a supply of *real* coins in it. Prepare an answer sheet, showing all possible combinations of coins for each jar.

The children place the proper coins in each bank. They use the answer sheet to check their work. (If the coins begin to disappear, revert to the use of play money.)

## 4. GO FLY A KITE!

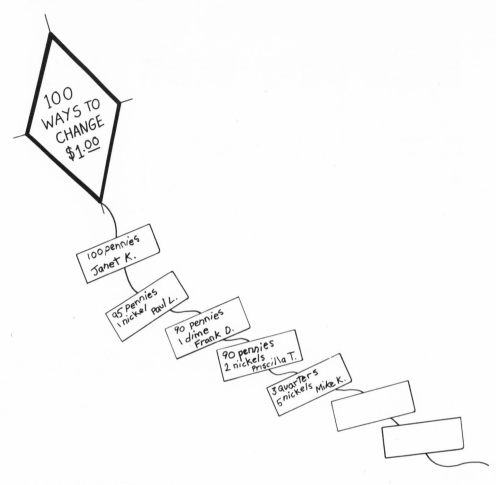

Hang a large construction paper kite on a wall near the learning center. Attach a string of blank "tail bows" cut from colorful construction paper.

Encourage children to think of different ways to make change for $1.00. When they have thought of ways which have not yet been used, they write their suggestions and their names on the bows. Keep adding bows to the kite tail until there are one hundred different ones. The children who made contributions win a penny for each suggestion made. (Actually there are 294 ways to change $1.00.)

## 5. STOREKEEPER GAME

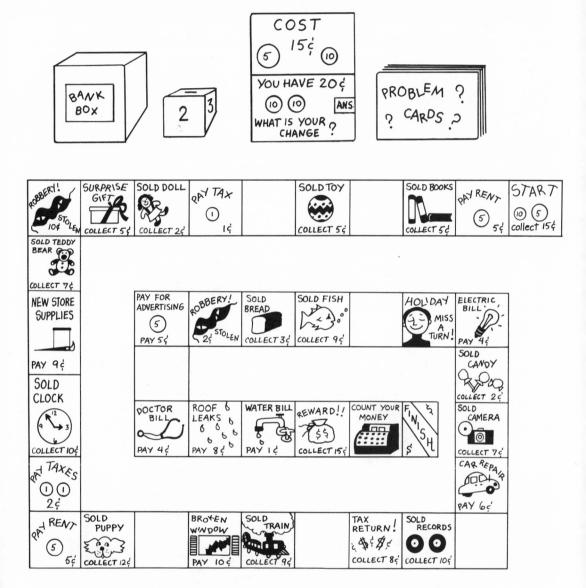

Construct a large game board as illustrated. Create a deck of game cards by writing a money problem (as in the example) on each card. Write the answer under a tab. Provide play money in a "Bank Box." A die should also be provided.

Each child selects a game marker and takes fifteen cents from the bank. The first player picks the top game card and must do the problem the card contains. If the answer is correct, the child rolls the cube in order to determine how many spaces to move. After moving the specified number of spaces, the child will do whatever is indicated in the box she lands on: She may collect money, pay a bill, or, in the case of landing on a blank space, do nothing.

If the child gives an incorrect answer to the problem card, she remains where she is until her next turn.

The children continue until all the players have reached the cash register at the end. The player with the most money at that time is the winner.

LEARNING CENTER NO. 12                    Level: GR. 2, 3

# Tick Tock Talk

Curriculum Area:   MATH, TELLING TIME

Goal:   PROMOTING SKILLS

Time concepts are among the most difficult for young children to master; they require a certain maturational level, as well as exposure to stimulating environmental experiences. Activities designed to promote the development of accurate time concepts should be as interesting as possible, while falling within the range of abilities of the students. Taking both these considerations into account, this center focuses upon the reinforcement of basic skills in telling time through the use of meaningful activities.

Individual and small-group learning experiences not only challenge children to practice telling time, but also motivate them to produce original solutions to creative problems.

## GAMES AND ACTIVITIES

### 1. TIME ON MY HANDS

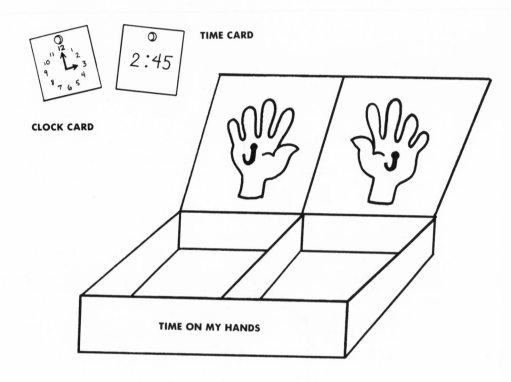

TIME CARD

CLOCK CARD

TIME ON MY HANDS

TIME ON MY HANDS SCORE SHEET

Name _____

Date _____

I got _____ right.

Divide a cigar box into two equal sections. In one section, place a number of "Clock Cards"—cards on which you have drawn a clock face with a fixed time. On the back of each card, under a flap, write the time the clock shows. In the other section, place a number of "Time Cards"—cards on which you have printed the times corresponding to the clock faces. Paste two colorful hands on the inside cover of the cigar box, and put a drapery hook into each. Run off score sheets.

The children are to hang a Clock Card on one hand, and the corresponding Time Card on the other. They check their work by looking at the answer on the back of the Clock Card. When they have completed all the cards, they record their results on the score sheet.

## 2. CLOCK-O

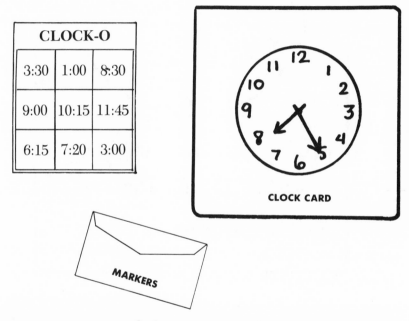

Prepare CLOCK-O cards by writing a time in each of nine squares on oaktag cards. Repeat some of the times on various cards, but make each card different. Prepare a clock face for each time designated on the cards. Put a batch of markers in an envelope.

The children play this game just like bingo. The caller (one of the students, or an aide) holds up a Clock Card for all to see. The players check their CLOCK-O cards to see if they have the time shown on the Clock Card. If they do, they place a marker on that space. The first player to cover up a straight line in any direction is the winner.

## 3. TIME NOTEBOOK

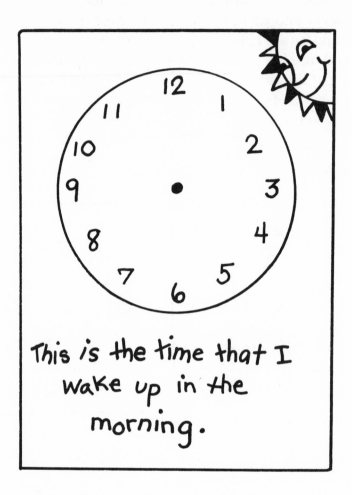

This is the time that I wake up in the morning.

Provide sheets of paper, each showing a clock with no hands. Each child is to make a personal notebook showing his time schedule during a typical school day. The children draw in the hands of the clock to show their various activities. For example, "I get up and get ready to go to school at 7:00." Other highlights of the day (e.g., lunch, gym, a favorite subject, etc.) are done in the same way on the additional sheets. Encourage the children to add little stories or draw pictures on the sheets that show their favorite activities.

## 4. FEEL THE TIME

Draw a clock face on heavy tagboard. Create numerals out of cardboard, heavy tinfoil, or pipe cleaners, and attach them to the clock face. The numerals should be raised enough so that they can be recognized by touch. Attach hands that are movable. Provide a supply of chips and a large kerchief.

Two children play this game together. One child sets the hands of the clock. The other child puts on a blindfold and tries to feel the time which was set by her partner. Turns are taken as the children alternate roles. They each get ten turns. For each correct answer, the player collects a chip. The player with the larger number of chips at the end of the game is the winner.

## 5. BEAT THE CLOCK

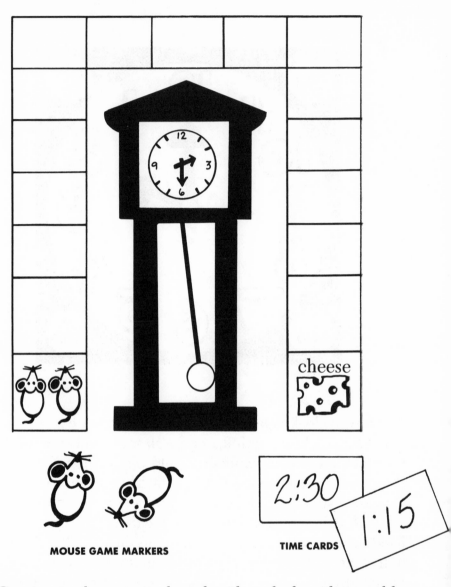

**MOUSE GAME MARKERS**

**TIME CARDS**

2:30

1:15

Construct a large game board with a clock with movable hands on it, as shown. Prepare a set of Time Cards, and provide a die and markers.

The players take turns choosing a Time Card and setting the hands of the clock to the appropriate time. They check each other's work. If correct, they roll a die to determine the number of spaces to move their marker. The first player to the finish line (the first mouse to reach the cheese) is the winner.

LEARNING CENTER NO. 13                Level: GR. 2 AND UP

# I Wish . . . I Wish . . . Storyland

Curriculum Area: LANGUAGE ARTS, WISHES

Goal: STIMULATING CREATIVITY, EXPLORING ATTITUDES AND VALUES

This center invites children to think and write about their wishes, hopes, and dreams. Children should be given complete freedom to write what they want, briefly or at length, to reveal themselves as little or as much as they are comfortable with. There are obviously no answers to be checked or evaluated. The material is personal and may disclose a great deal about the children's self images and value systems. The teacher will have to exercise judgment in devising ways to use or follow up this activity. Some children may enjoy showing their creations to others in small groups and sharing their reactions and thoughts. Some children may want to talk only to the teacher about their work. Each child's unique contribution should be accepted as individually worthy.

## GAMES AND ACTIVITIES

## 1. WISHING WELL

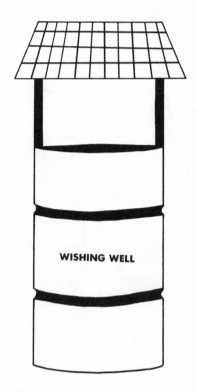

Construct a "Wishing Well" by covering a large coffee can with construction paper. Make a canopy out of construction paper or cloth pasted to cardboard, and glue it to dowels that you have taped inside the can.

Write a series of sentence starters for wishes on index cards. For example, "When my friends talk about me, I wish they would say . . . " or "If I could change my name, I would change it to . . . " Put the index cards in the well.

The children are to reach into the well and pull out a wish. They are to complete the sentence and write a story explaining further. It can be a serious story, a funny story, or a fantasy, as the child chooses. The children may choose to write their names on their stories or not. They may post their stories on the Wishing Bulletin Board, signed or unsigned. Or, if they prefer, they may put their stories in their folders to show to the teacher.

## 2. I WISH CARTOONS

I WISH I DIDN'T        I WISH I COULD        I WISH I HAD

Prepare many copies of several different dittoes, each showing a person in a different mood. Have the children choose one (or more, if they wish) of the dittoes and write a story to complete the wish each character has begun to express.

## 3. I WISH I WAS

Place a number of magazines at the center. Have the children look through the magazines, and have each child choose a picture of any famous person she would like to be if she weren't herself. Each child cuts out the picture of the person, pastes it on a sheet of writing paper, and tells a story of an experience she imagines she would have if she were that famous person.

LEARNING CENTER NO. 14             Level: GR. 2—4

# Quiet Area . . . Scientist At Work

Curriculum Area:   SCIENCE, EXPERIMENTING

Goal:   PROMOTING CONCEPTS

Children of all ages are extremely interested in exploring the natural wonders they meet in their growing lives. This center provides activities that capitalize on this strong interest. The children use a variety of materials to carry out investigations designed to make them aware of the scientific phenomena in their environment. The center does not concentrate on one topic, but rather focuses on the scientific method of inquiry, involving formulating questions and hypotheses, experimenting, observing, recording, and generalizing results.

There are twenty-six simple experiments in this center—one for each letter of the alphabet. Most of them end with an open-ended question that invites the learner to go beyond the actual results of the investigation.

## GAMES AND ACTIVITIES

### ABC'S OF SCIENCE

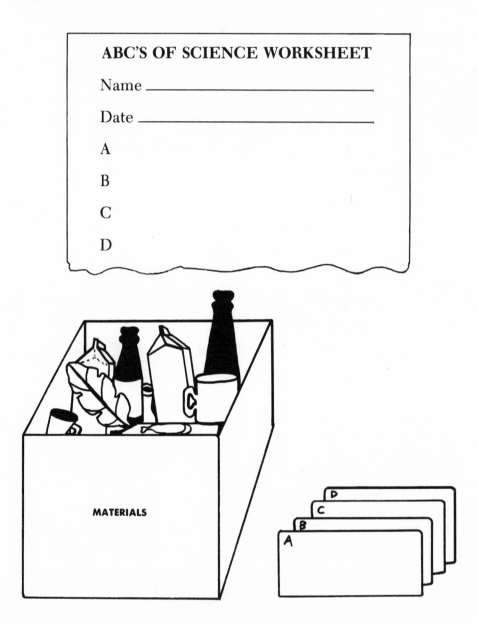

**ABC'S OF SCIENCE WORKSHEET**

Name _____

Date _____

A

B

C

D

MATERIALS

Choose twenty-six topics for experimentation, from A to Z. Organize a large box with the materials the children will need for these experiments. Prepare twenty-six large cards, writing directions to follow for each experiment. Provide worksheets

lettered from A to Z on which children record the results of each experiment. Instruct children to follow the directions for each experiment, recording their observations. When they have finished, they are to put their worksheets in a box at the center. When there are four or five worksheets in a box, arrange for these four or five students to meet together and discuss their work.

**A—AIR**

Can you lift a book without touching it? Put a book on a balloon and blow into the balloon. When you have enough air in the balloon it will be strong enough to lift the book.

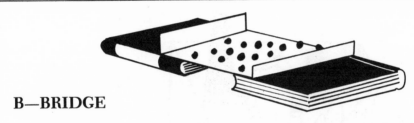

**B—BRIDGE**

Place a sheet of paper flat across two books to make a bridge. See how many pebbles the paper will hold without collapsing. Now fold the sides of the paper up. Put the paper across the two books again.

Now how many pebbles will it hold?

**C—CLOCK**

Fill a glass with water. Place a clock behind the glass. What happened to the size of the numerals and lines on the clock?

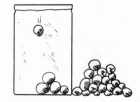

## D—DROP

Fill a glass to the top with water. Drop a pebble in. Did the water spill over? Guess how many more pebbles it will take before the water spills over. Then try it and see. Have a guessing contest with your friends.

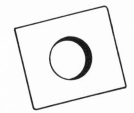

## E—EYES

Test your eyes to see which one you favor. Look at something small on a far away wall. Now take a frame and with both your eyes open look through the hole at the same small object on the wall.

Now close one eye and look through the frame with the other eye. What happened?

Now try the other eye. What happened?

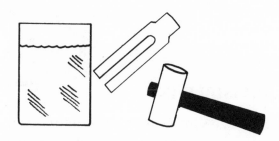

## F—FORK

Fill a glass with water. Hit the tuning fork with the mallet. Put the tuning fork into the glass of water. What happened?

## G—GROW

Put some soil in a carton. Plant three beans in the soil. Label the carton with your name and with the planting date. Place the carton in a sunny place and keep the soil moist. How long do you think it will take for the plant to grow an inch tall? Wait about a week and look to see how big the plant grew.

## H—HOUSE

Stare at this house for one minute. Now look at a blank wall. What do you see?

## I—INVISIBLE INK

Squeeze some lemon juice into a dish. Take a sheet of paper and dip a toothpick into the lemon juice to write your friend an invisible message. Have your friend place the paper under a lamp and wait until the paper gets warm. What happened?

**J—JET PLANE**

Blow up a balloon. Let go of the end. What happened to the balloon?

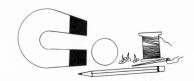

**K—KNOCK**

Knock on the desk, the floor, the wall, a book, the window, and any other object you choose. Do they all sound the same or different. Why?

**L—LEAVES**

Place a sheet of carbon paper face-down on a sheet of white paper. Place a leaf on top of the carbon paper and hit it with a mallet. What do you see on the white paper?

**M—MAGNET**

At random, pick about five different small objects out of the box and place them on the table. Touch a magnet to each one. What happened? Try five more objects, deliberately choosing the ones you want. What happened?

## N—NAIL

Put some water in a dish and put a nail in the water. What will happen? Wait a few days. What happened?

## O—OIL

Put a few drops of cooking oil into a glass of water. What happened to the oil?

## P—PENNIES

Put about five tablespoons of vinegar and one teaspoon of salt into a cup. Mix them well. Put five dirty pennies into the cup. What do you think will happen?

Leave them in for one full day. What did the pennies look like when you took them out?

## Q—QUARTER

Put a quarter under a sheet of paper. Rub the lead of your pencil across the paper over the quarter. What do you see?

Try the same thing with other objects.

**R—RING**

Put a different amount of water in each of four glasses. Tap each glass with your pencil. Do they all make the same ringing sound?

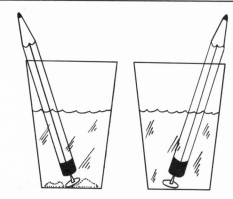

**S—SALT WATER**

Fill two glasses with water. Put two tablespoons of salt in one of the glasses. Stick thumb tacks into the erasers of two different pencils. Place one pencil (eraser down) into the plain water and the other pencil into the salt water.

What happened to each thumb tack?

 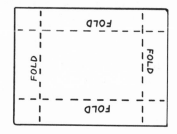

**T—TACKS**

Get a piece of aluminum foil. Fold the sides up to form a box. Put water in a large pan. Put your aluminum box-boat in the water and load it up with tacks. How many will it carry before sinking?

Try folding another piece of foil in a different shape and repeat the experiment. Which shape holds the most tacks?

## U—UNDER

Blow up a small balloon. Fill a basin or the sink with water. Hold the balloon on the water. Now push it down slowly. What happens as you try to push it completely under?

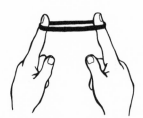

## V—VIBRATE

Stretch a rubber band between your hands. Have a friend pluck it. Can you see it vibrate?

Now stretch the rubber band out tighter. Can you still see it vibrate? How did the sound change?

Try stretching the rubber band different ways to make different sounds until you can play a little song.

## W—WATER

Put some water in a glass. Put a rubber band around the glass to mark the top of the water line. Leave the water in the glass for one full day. What happened?

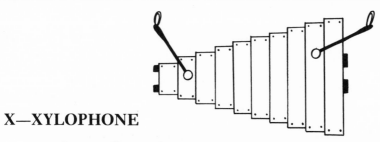

## X—XYLOPHONE

Use the small wooden hammer to hit one long bar and one short bar of the xylophone. Which one makes the lower sound?

## Y—YOURSELF

Fill a glass with water. Look at yourself in a mirror through the glass of water. What do you see?

## Z—ZIG-ZAG

Take a small round balloon out of the box and draw a zig-zag shape on it with a felt tip pen. Ask your friend to guess what the zig-zag shape will look like when you blow up the balloon. You guess, too. Were you both right?

LEARNING CENTER NO. 15                                    Level: GR. 2-5

# Look At Me!

Curriculum Area:  LANGUAGE ARTS, WRITING ABOUT SELF

Goal:  PROMOTING CREATIVE SELF-EXPRESSION, GROWTH IN
VALUES AND ATTITUDES

The activities at this center will help children get to know themselves and each other better. They share facts, feelings, and experiences, and they become aware of how they see themselves, how they see others, and how others see them. They develop a sense and a respect for the uniqueness of each human being. Some of the material that emerges may become highly personal, and the teacher will exercise judgment about how to use and share it.

## GAMES AND ACTIVITIES

### 1. I AM ME

**PHOTO OF CHILD**

I am _____ .

I am _____ years old.

My address is _____ .

and my phone number is _____ .

My favorites:

Hobby _____        Color _____

Sport _____        Book _____

Food _____        Animal _____

My pet peeve is _____ .

Take a photograph of each child. Provide copies of a data sheet, as shown in the illustration. Each child completes the information on the data sheet and pastes his picture at the top. The children hang their completed data sheets in the classroom for others to read and discuss.

This activitiy must be completed before Activity Two is begun.

## 2. WHO AM I?

MYSTERY GUEST #1

MYSTERY GUEST #2

MYSTERY GUEST #3

MYSTERY GUEST #4

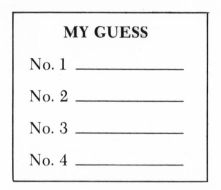

MY GUESS

No. 1 _____

No. 2 _____

No. 3 _____

No. 4 _____

Provide a supply of white construction paper and magic markers. Instruct the children to use a strong flashlight or the light from the overhead projector to make a silhouette. To do this, one child sits in a chair between the strong light and a wall on which the construction paper has been tacked. Another child traces the silhouetted profile on the construction paper. Then they switch positions. When they both have a profile, they draw or paste pictures on them to represent the information contained in their data sheets (in Activity One).

Each day, display three or four completed profile silhouettes on the center background. Number them, and have the children examine the silhouettes and guess who each may be. Guesses may be written on voting sheets. At the end of the day, reveal whose silhouettes were displayed and see how many correct guesses were made on the voting sheets.

## 3. MY MOOD BOOK

HAPPY        SAD        ANGRY        SILLY        AFRAID

In a box or envelope, put strips of paper identifying many different moods: happy, sad, angry, silly, afraid, disappointed, excited, nervous, frustrated. In another box, put a supply of white paper and cardboard picture frames. The child chooses a mood word and draws a picture of himself showing how he looks when he is in that mood. He pastes the picture in the frame, then he writes a little story telling about a time he was in that mood. After the child has done a few such mood stories, he can combine them into a book by punching holes and using paper fasteners or yarn, and making a cover, title page, and Table of Contents. Display the children's books in the classroom for everybody to read.

## 4. "ME" RECIPES

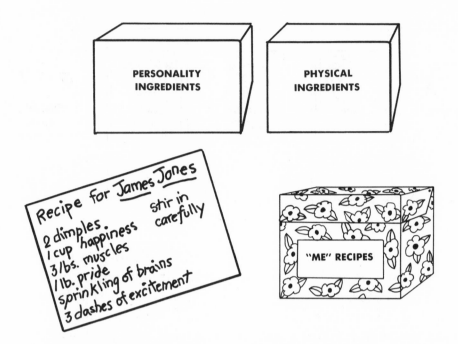

In this activity, children are encouraged to think about the characteristics which make them the persons they are. In one box, labeled "Physical Ingredients," provide index cards on which you have written various physical characteristics: height, weight, strength, physical skills and talents (e.g., swimming, singing), special features (e.g., double-jointedness, freckles), voice, pace, etc. In another box, labeled "Personality Ingredients," identify various personality traits on index cards: cheerful, proud, enthusiastic, energetic, temperamental, fun-loving, ambitious, creative, sensitive, sympathetic, etc.

The children examine the words in each box. They choose the general characteristics that they think best describe them and think about the degree to which they possess each characteristic.

These ingredients are then creatively formed into a "Me" Recipe which describes what is needed in order to make another "Me." The children write their recipes on blank index cards and put them in the "Me" Recipe box. Later, the class can form small groups and members can share and discuss their recipes with each other.

## 5. MY COAT OF ARMS

Prepare dittoed coats of arms, as illustrated. In each section, children are to draw pictures or symbols, or write words, phrases, or sentences in response to questions you suggest.

*For example:*

1. What three things are you good at in school?

2. What is one thing that you like most to do in our school?

3. What would you like most to change or improve about yourself at school?

4. What is one thing your classmates admire about you?

5. What one thing can your friends do to make you happy in school?

6. What has been your greatest accomplishment in school?

LEARNING CENTER NO. 16                              Level: GR. 3

## And They Lived Happily Ever After . . . Or Did They?

Curriculum Area:   READING, FAIRY TALES

Goal:   PROMOTING CONCEPTS, IMAGINATION, CREATIVITY

Young children are naturally imaginative and serve as a vast source of untapped creativity. This center stimulates the children to share the wealth of their imaginations through delightful tasks related to fairy tales. Fairy tales are enjoyed by almost all young children because of their fanciful plots. Taking off on this characteristic, this center helps children to recognize the elements of fairy tales, and to apply these elements to their own creative story writing.

## GAMES AND ACTIVITIES

## 1. POT OF GOLD

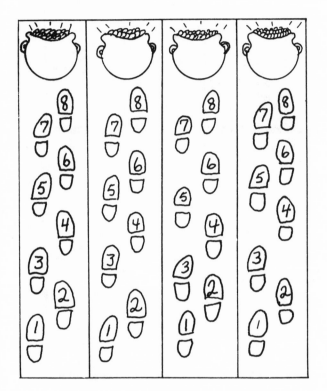

A little girl
walked to her
grandmother's house.

**FAIRY TALE CARDS**

Create a game board, as in the illustration. Make up a deck of 5″ x 8″ cards by writing an event that occurred in a popular fairy tale on each card. Place the cards face down next to the game board.

Four children may play together. They place their markers on the first step of the game board. The first player turns over the top Fairy Tale Card and reads it so that all players can hear. She must then name the fairy tale in which the event described occurred. If all players agree that the answer is correct, she moves one step toward the pot of gold. If the answer is incorrect, the player returns the card to the bottom of the deck and remains where she is. The first player to reach the pot of gold is the winner.

## 2. ANALYZE A FAIRY TALE

Provide a number of simple fairy tale books. Make six large tagboard posters, as illustrated, each identifying an important element of fairy tales. Put a box in front of each poster.

The children are to choose a fairy tale, read it, and illustrate each of the elements of that fairy tale. The illustrations are placed in the boxes beneath each poster.

## 3. DID THEY REALLY?

The children are to choose one of the fairy tales at the center. After reading it, they are to look into the crystal ball and imagine what might have happened "after they lived happily ever after." Provide sample story endings, and encourage the children to be as funny, imaginative, outrageous as they can. Provide crystal ball writing paper and have the children write their stories in the crystal ball and post the papers at the center.

**CRYSTAL BALL
WRITING PAPER**

*Sample story:*

---

### JACK AND THE BEANSTALK

The giant fell down dead and everyone lived happily ever after. But . . . did they really???

The dead giant began to smell and the neighbors all began to complain. Jack's family had to give the giant a decent funeral, but it cost a fortune to bury a giant! Poor Jack worked the goose overtime until it finally died of exhaustion. Jack had just enough golden eggs to pay for the funeral. The family was poor all over again.

---

## 4. MY OWN FAIRY TALE

The boy who wanted to be king.

The little princess that no one loved.

**MAGIC PUMPKIN**

Provide fairy tale starters for the children by writing provocative situations on paper. Fold the papers and place them in a plastic Halloween pumpkin.

The child draws out a story starter and composes a modern fairy tale, pretending the event is taking place in today's world.

The following sample story was written in response to the story starter: "Your class is helped by a beautiful princess."

---

### SAMANTHA
#### by Lucy G.

Once upon a time, there lived a heartless teacher who gave her class a mountain of homework to do every night. One day the whole class wrote a letter to Samantha, the beautiful fairy princess, and told her about the teacher. Samantha came to school one day in the disguise of a substitute teacher. She put a magic potion into the teacher's milk during lunch. All of a sudden a warm glow came over the teacher.

From that day on, the children never had to take school work home.

---

LEARNING CENTER NO. 17                    Level: GR. 3, 4

# Decoding Multiplication Facts

Curriculum Area:   MATH, MULTIPLICATION

Goal:   PROMOTING SKILLS

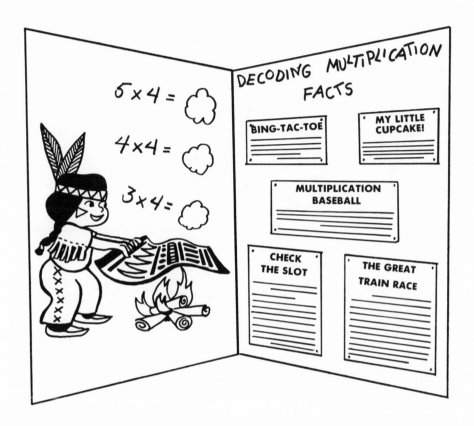

It takes a lot of practice to commit multiplication facts to memory. The activities at this center motivate children to use multiplication facts quickly and accurately by making these skills the means to a desirable end—playing and winning games.

## GAMES AND ACTIVITIES

### 1. BING-TAC-TOE

| X | 1 | 2 | 3 | 4 | 5 | 6 |
|---|---|---|---|---|---|---|
| 1 | 1 | 2 | 3 | 4 | 5 | 6 |
| 2 | 2 | 4 | 6 | 8 | 10 | 12 |
| 3 | 3 | 6 | 9 | 12 | 15 | 18 |
| 4 | 4 | 8 | 12 | 16 | 20 | 24 |
| 5 | 5 | 10 | 15 | 20 | 25 | 30 |
| 6 | 6 | 12 | 18 | 24 | 30 | 36 |

| X | 7 | 8 | 9 | 10 | 11 | 12 |
|---|---|---|---|---|---|---|
| 7 | 49 | 56 | 63 | 70 | 77 | 84 |
| 8 | 56 | 64 | 72 | 80 | 88 | 96 |
| 9 | 63 | 72 | 81 | 90 | 99 | 108 |
| 10 | 70 | 80 | 90 | 100 | 110 | 120 |
| 11 | 77 | 88 | 99 | 110 | 121 | 132 |
| 12 | 84 | 96 | 108 | 120 | 132 | 144 |

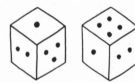  

Make two sets of dice out of foam rubber. On one set, put from seven to twelve dots on each face. Make two separate 14"x 14" game boards, as in the illustration. In the corner of each two-inch square box, put the answer under a flap. Make a number of two-inch markers out of construction paper of two colors, so that the players can each use a different color.

Two children play together. The players decide whether they want to use the one to six game board or the seven to twelve board. They put the board on a table or on the floor. The first player rolls the dice, multiplies the two numbers, calls out the answer, and then checks the answer by looking under the flap of the square corresponding to the roll. If correct, she places a colored marker on the square. The play continues in this way until one child has filled in one solid line across, down, or diagonally.

## 2. MULTIPLICATION BASEBALL

| 1 | 2 | 3 | 4 | 5 | 6 | 7 | 8 | 9 | TOTAL |
|---|---|---|---|---|---|---|---|---|-------|
| 2 [2] | 12 [6] | 15 [5] |   |   |   |   |   |   |       |

| 1 | 2 | 3 | 4 | 5 | 6 | 7 | 8 | 9 | TOTAL |
|---|---|---|---|---|---|---|---|---|-------|
| 4 [4] | 6 [3] |   |   |   |   |   |   |   |       |

Xerox a number of scoreboards, as in the illustration, so that each player has her own score sheet. Construct a spinner with the numerals one through eight.

Two children play this game. They score runs this way: For the first inning, the score is the number on the spinner times one, for the second inning, the score is the number on the spinner times two, and so on for nine innings. Each player spins the arrow, records the number in the upper right-hand corner of the box, does the multiplication, and records the score in the box. Players add up their scores at the end to see who won. The scores will be extremely high, but so will the interest.

## 3. MY LITTLE CUPCAKE!

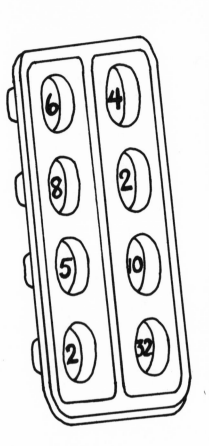

| CUPCAKE SCORE SHEET | |
|---|---|
| Round | Score |
| 1 | |
| 2 | |
| 3 | |
| 4 | |
| 5 | |
| 6 | |
| 7 | |
| 8 | |
| 9 | |
| 10 | |
| Total | |

Paint a number on the bottom of each section of an old cupcake pan. Prepare individual score sheets for the players.

The player should stand about two or three feet from the pan and toss a soft rubber eraser into one of the cups. He tells two factors which will make the number in the section where the eraser landed. The players check each other's answers. In case of disagreement, they check with the teacher or consult the multiplication table. If correct, the player records the number tossed on his score sheet. If incorrect, he scores zero for that round. At the end of ten tosses, the child with the highest total is the winner.

## 4. THE GREAT TRAIN RACE

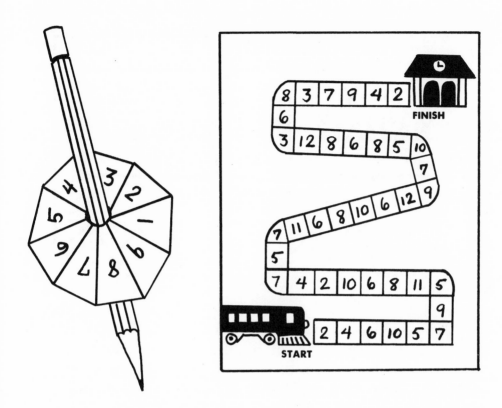

Make a game board on a large sheet of tagboard by marking off squares to create an irregular track pattern. Draw a train to indicate the "Start," and a train station to indicate the "Finish." Randomly, write numbers from one through twelve in each square. Make a spinner from a nine-sided piece of cardboard about five inches in diameter. Number each section from one through nine. Push a pencil through the center.

The players take turns spinning. If the spinner comes to rest on an odd number, the player moves one space on the board. If the spinner comes to rest on an even number, she moves two spaces. In order to stay in that space, the player must multiply the number on the spinner by the number on the space. If correct, she stays. If incorrect, she returns to her original space and waits for her next turn. The first player to reach the train station is the winner. Players check each other's answers, consulting the teacher or aide in case of disagreement.

## 5. CHECK THE SLOT

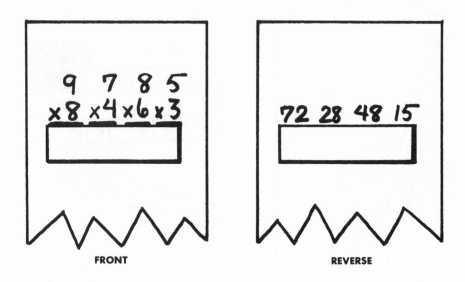

FRONT                                      REVERSE

Write multiplication problems across a sheet of 9″ x 12″ tagboard. Below the row of problems, where the answers normally would be placed, cut out a long strip creating a window. On the reverse side of the tagboard, just above the slot or window, write the answers to each problem.

The children place the tagboard over a sheet of writing paper. They solve each problem, writing their answers in the slots so that they appear only on the writing paper. When finished, they turn the tagboard over, and they can easily and instantly tell if their answers are right or wrong.

LEARNING CENTER NO. 18                     Level: GR. 3,4

# The Professor's Sentence Puzzlers

Curriculum Area:   LANGUAGE ARTS, SYNTAX, SENTENCE FORMS
Goal:   PROMOTING SKILLS, CONCEPTS

Recognizing correct sentence patterns has been an area of grammar instruction that has relied heavily upon the use of repetitive textbook drill. At this center, students are offered enjoyable games and manipulative activities as an alternative means of developing related skills. By participating in this center, children are not only learning in a more interesting and enjoyable way, but they are also acquiring a functional rather than merely intellectual understanding of the nature and role of different parts of speech, of word order, and of the different sentence forms.

## GAMES AND ACTIVITIES

### 1. WORD TOSS

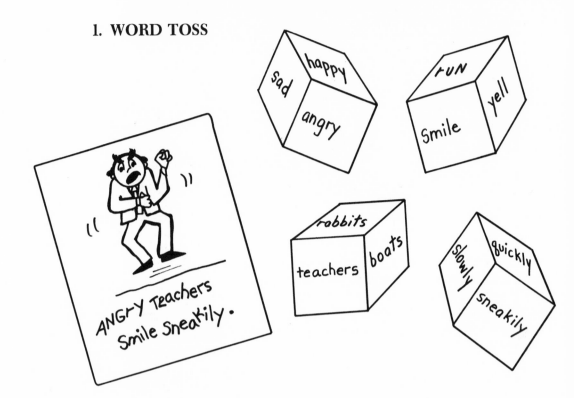

Create four large dice by covering foam rubber squares with fabric. Make sure each die is a different color, since each die will represent a different part of speech. Tape a word to each surface of the die, using only adjectives on the first die, nouns on the second, verbs on the third, and adverbs on the fourth. The child rolls the dice (color by color, as specified in your directions) and writes the resulting sentence on a sheet of drawing paper. He then illustrates the sentence he made.

Additional parts of speech can be added or substituted (e.g., "where" phrases) if you so desire.

## 2. CARTOON SORT

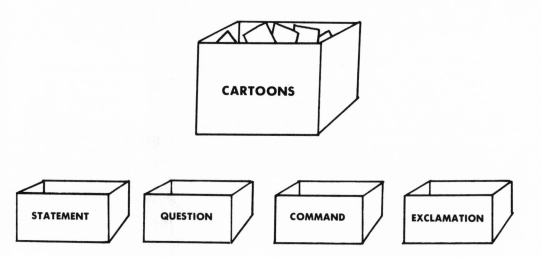

Find cartoons in newspapers or magazines that contain one-sentence captions illustrating the various sentence types. Mount each cartoon on colorful construction paper. On the back of each card, put an answer code in a square:

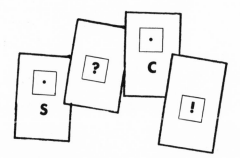

Laminate the cards, or cover with clear contact paper.

Children are to take a cartoon card from the large box, read it, and sort the card into the box which identifies the kind of sentence which is used in the caption. They check their work by looking at the symbols on the backs of the cartoon cards.

## 3. SCRAMBLED EGGS

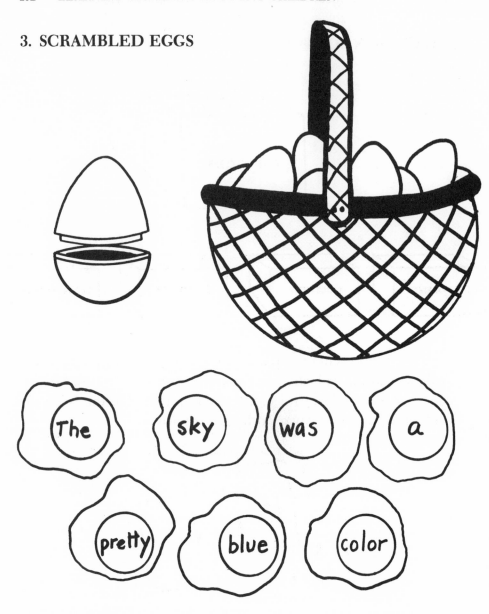

Use plastic egg-shaped hose containers for this activity. Prepare sentences for each container by writing each separate word on a piece of white and yellow cardboard to resemble a fried egg. Number the backs to provide the answer sequence. Mix the words up and put them in the egg. Place all egg containers in a large basket.

The children are to select a container, spill out the words, and arrange them so that the sentence makes sense. They check the backs to see if they are right.

## 4. BEAN BAG TOSS

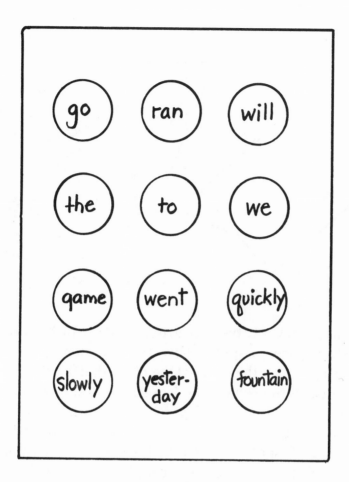

Using tagboard, prepare a large game board that can be placed on the floor. Cut circles out of construction paper and tape them to the board. Write words of different parts of speech on each circle.

Children take turns tossing a bean bag onto a word. Each child keeps a record of the words she lands on. All words accumulated by a player must be used by that player. The first player to construct a complete sentence is the winner.

## 5. SENTENCE RUMMY

Prepare a set of fifty-two cards on which words representing the various parts of speech have been written. Three or four children may play this game. One child shuffles the cards and deals six cards to each player, leaving the rest of the deck face down on the table. Each player is to try to make a complete sentence using all the cards in her hand. If nobody has a sentence, the first player discards (face up) one card and selects the top card from the pile. The next player may either select the previous player's discard or the next card from the pile. She then must discard one card. The players continue in turn until someone can make a complete six word sentence.

LEARNING CENTER NO. 19                              Level: GR. 4

# Mother Nature's Children

Curriculum Area:  SCIENCE, ANIMAL LIFE
              Goal:  CONCEPT DEVELOPMENT

At this center, the children learn about the habits and habitats of different kinds of animals. Simple ecological concepts are graphically illustrated. The children use the scientist's method of direct observation, combined with research and reading. The center should be stocked with books on animal life, as well as with the materials the children will need to carry out the tasks.

## GAMES AND ACTIVITIES

## 1. MINIZOO

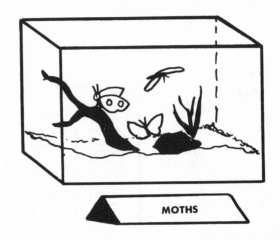

MOTHS

**FEEDING CHART**
1. FRUIT
2. LEAVES
3. COOKED EGGS
4. A BIT OF HAMBURGER
5. FLIES

**MINIZOOKEEPER'S CHART**
(ANT CAGE)

MAY 10- CLASS CAPTURED
25 ANTS
MAY 13- FED THE ANTS
TINY PIECES OF
DRIED BREAD
MAY 14- ANTS BEGAN TO
TUNNEL INTO
THE EARTH

Use old aquariums or other suitable enclosures in which to confine tiny captured animals. Place a half-inch of plaster of paris in the bottom of each container, covered by layers of aquarium gravel, coarse sand, and topsoil.

Have the children search the environment around the school, hunting for centipedes, spiders, grasshoppers, butterflies, moths, etc., to bring back to the classroom and to the learning center.

Children should then research the characteristics and proper care of their new zoo inhabitants and record this information near each cage. In addition, hang sheets in the learning center on which children can record observed living habits of each animal.

## 2. HOME SWEET HOME

FOREST ANIMALS

Place small cardboard boxes in the learning center, which children can use to construct dioramas to show the natural environments of various animals. Have pictures of many different animals or provide rubber animal models. The children may select one animal or a group of animals that live in the same natural environment. They may use the books available at the center to research the subject. Then they design different natural habitats for their chosen animals, creating dioramas and identifying them by labeling them Forest Animals, Jungle Animals, City Animals, Ocean Animals, Desert Animals, Underground Animals, Mountain Animals, River Animals, etc.

## 3. FOOD CHAINS

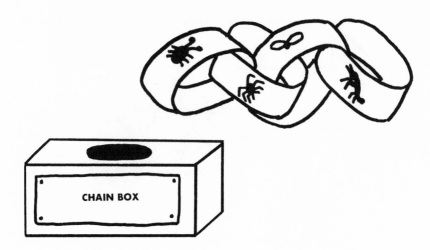

After children have had work on food chains and understand how they help maintain a balance in nature, some children may be interested in making their own food chains.

Prepare starter links: Make chain links out of construction paper and on each link draw or paste a picture of some animal. The child is to reach into the Chain Box for a starter link. She is then to create her own construction paper link and draw on it either a picture of an organism which lives off the animal on the starter link, or a picture of an organism on which the starter link organism lives. She continues to create links for both ends of the chain until ideas are exhausted. For example, one child reached into the Chain Box and drew out a link with a picture of a spider. She then created a link with a picture of a fly to show what a spider eats. Then she made a link with a picture of a praying mantis to show what may eat a spider, and another link with a bird to show what the mantis might be eaten by. She continued making links that would attach to either end of the spider, showing the progression of natural events.

When the child completes the links, she attaches them all together to form a food chain. Each individually constructed food chain may be displayed near the learning center.

## 4. FAMOUS ANIMALS PARADE

ANIMALS WHO BEHAVE
AS ANIMALS

Lassie is a
famous dog who
saved Timmy.

ANIMALS WHO BEHAVE
AS HUMANS

Smokey the Bear warns
us about how to
avoid forest fires.

Construct two large, fancy parade floats out of posterboard and display them at the learning center. Label one float "Animals Who Behave as Animals," and the other float "Animals Who Behave as Humans." The children select a famous animal they know about from literature, television, or the movies. They draw a picture of the animal they selected and write a brief identifying statement about the animal. They place their illustrations and statements on the appropriate parade float. When the floats become crowded, additional floats may be constructed if childrens' interests dictate.

## 5. WHO AM I?

Cut out pictures of animals from coloring books. Color them and place them in a box or envelope. Make silhouetted outlines of all the same animals. Stand a three-paneled bulletin board on a table. Divide it into various categories, such as, River Animals, Forest Animals, City Animals. Mount the silhouettes in their appropriate places on the bulletin board. On index cards, write clues, such as, "I am a large animal who loves to eat honey."

Children match the colored pictures to the mounted silhouettes, and then place the clues under the appropriate animal's picture.

LEARNING CENTER NO. 20                         Level: GR. 4

## Undersea Adventures

Curriculum Area:  LANGUAGE ARTS, IMAGINARY SEA STORIES
Goal:  PROMOTING CREATIVE WRITING

Most children enjoy exciting stories about the "deep." Before creating this center, the teacher will have introduced the children to sea stories in library books and basal readers. This center gives children various stimuli to inspire them to try their own hand at story telling. Some of the activities call for description, some for plotting; some provide structure, others give the child's imagination free reign. The children will enjoy sharing their creations with each other.

## GAMES AND ACTIVITIES

## 1. PORTHOLE STORIES

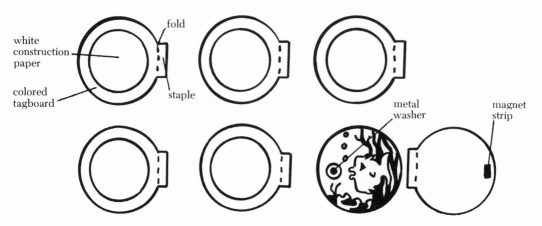

PORTHOLE OPENED WITH PICTURE EXPOSED

The teacher will construct a bulletin board with six portholes, each containing a hidden underwater scene. The children are to open any one of the portholes and write a description or story based upon the scene revealed.

To make the portholes, cut six circles (six to seven inches in diameter) out of colored construction paper. On each circle, paste a drawn picture or a magazine illustration of an underwater scene. Mount the six pictures on a bulletin board.

Using colored tagboard, cut out six more circles of the same size, but leave a one-inch tab extending out of the circle. Glue a small magnet strip to each tagboard circle just opposite the tab. Also glue a metal washer to each construction paper circle with the underwater scene.

Cut out six smaller circles (four to five inches in diameter) using white construction paper. Paste the white circles on the backs of the tagboard circles, to give the appearance of glass in a porthole. Staple the tab of each tagboard circle to the bulletin board so that it covers the underwater scene. The white construction paper should be on the outside of the porthole, and the magnet strip on the tagboard should meet the metal washer on the picture to close the porthole.

## 2. STORY WHEEL

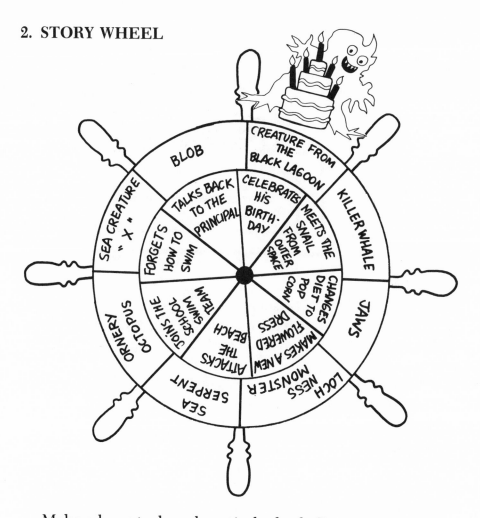

Make a large tagboard nautical wheel. Cut out two circles, one larger than the other. Divide each of them into eight segments. Around the rim of the outer circle, write the names of denizens of the deep. (Some may be well known, such as Jaws and the Loch Ness Monster; some you create yourself.) In the segments of the inner circle, briefly describe some imaginary, provocative action, such as "forgets how to swim." You may add an illustration to each segment, or you may have the children make their own illustrations for the characters. Attach the two circles by putting a metal fastener through the middle.

The child spins the outside wheel, chooses a resulting story title, and writes a creative story based on the title. Stories can be collected and organized into a class anthology, *Stories from the Deep*.

### 3. KING NEPTUNE'S SECRET

Collect small objects (such as sea shells, snorkels, toy boats and fish) which represent life on or in the sea. Add some objects which are not usually associated with the sea (such as a badge, a quarter, a whistle, an earring). Place them in a box. Cover the box. The child reaches into the box and brings out three or four objects. He is to write a short, creative story using these objects.

The teacher may guide the children toward creative writing by placing these directions on the cover of the box:

1. Slowly reach your hand into the box and bring out the first object you touch. Look at the object carefully. Think about what secret it might reveal. Put it down in front of you.

2. Repeat this procedure until you have brought out about three or four objects.

3. Try to arrange the objects in front of you so that they might be telling a story.

4. Write your story on a paper. Feel free to add pictures if you want.

## 4. HIDDEN TREASURES

Write story starters on 3″ x 5″ cards and place them in a file box decorated as a treasure chest, and labeled "Hidden Treasures."

*Sample story starters:*

---

"I wish I could leave this aquarium," sighed Sally Goldfish as she longingly watched the children playing in the classroom. "If only I could rejoin my brothers and sisters back in the pond. Why, I remember when . . . "

---

"Are you awake yet?" Charlie Tuna anxiously asked his father. "Don't forget that today you promised to . . . "

---

Ollie Octopus had decided to explore some new watery neighborhoods. He had great fun until he realized that it was an hour swim back to his home and only a half-hour of daylight remained!

---

Benny the Bluefish had been hiding in an underwater cave for two hours when . . .

The child chooses a starter card and completes the story. Provide a bulletin board designated as King Neptune's Treasures. Have a supply of tagboard or construction paper so the children can make frames for their stories and display them on the bulletin board.

LEARNING CENTER NO. 21                      Level: GR. 4, 5

## Nutty Times

Curriculum Area:  MATH, ESTIMATING, LANGUAGE ARTS, RESEARCH, CREATIVE WRITING

Goal:  PROMOTING SKILLS, CONCEPTS, AND CREATIVITY

   The activities at this center all revolve around a central theme of high interest—nuts. Each activity deals with a different aspect of this interesting topic, thus allowing children to combine the exercise of skills and concepts with the use of imagination and humor. Children practice estimating weight and number, making charts, doing direct research, and doing research in reference sources. Finally, they are invited to be creative, using colloquial language to make up a story as realistic or fantastic as they wish.

## GAMES AND ACTIVITIES

### 1. WEIGHING AWAY

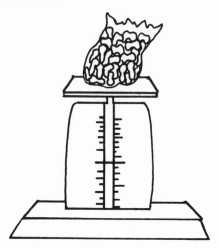

Provide bags of nuts of all kinds and a scale. Prepare data sheets for the children to use.

| Nut | Estimated Weight | Actual Weight | One nut weighs | |
|---|---|---|---|---|
| | | | About | Exactly |
| 10 Walnuts | | | | |
| 10 Pistachios | | | | |
| 10 Peanuts | | | | |
| 10 Brazil Nuts | | | | |
| 10 Pecans | | | | |

First the children estimate the weight of the various groups of ten nuts. They record their estimates on the data sheets, and then they check their estimates by weighing each group of nuts.

Finally, have them try to guess the weight of one nut in each group. Once they have recorded their estimates (which should, of course, be about one tenth of the actual weight recorded for the group of ten), they check by weighing the nut.

## 2. NUTTY JARS

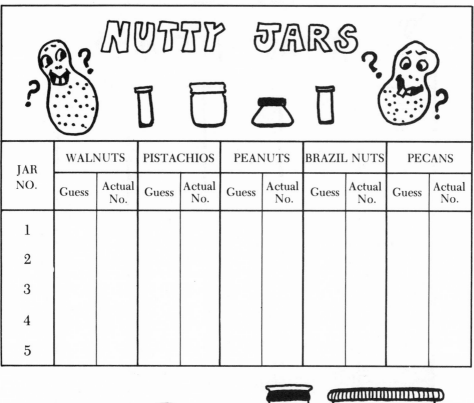

| JAR NO. | WALNUTS | | PISTACHIOS | | PEANUTS | | BRAZIL NUTS | | PECANS | |
|---|---|---|---|---|---|---|---|---|---|---|
| | Guess | Actual No. | Guess | Actual No. | Guess | Actual No. | Guess | Actual No. | Guess | Actual No. |
| 1 | | | | | | | | | | |
| 2 | | | | | | | | | | |
| 3 | | | | | | | | | | |
| 4 | | | | | | | | | | |
| 5 | | | | | | | | | | |

Collect five jars, each of a different volume. The children estimate the number of nuts of different kinds each jar will hold. They write their estimates on the data sheet. Then they check the estimates by actually filling each jar with the different kinds of nuts.

## 3. OUR FAVORITE NUT

Have enough nuts so that all the children can eat one of each type and decide which they like best. Give the children rectangular pieces of construction paper of different colors. A large, colorful class tagboard graph is constructed, as the children place their pieces of construction paper in the columns for their favorite nuts. When the graph is completed, conduct a group discussion of the results.

## 4. NUTTY RESEARCH

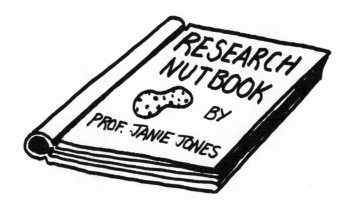

Provide research materials (encyclopedias, library books, etc.) for the children. Each child selects a nut which is especially interesting to him and researches such information as:

Where is it grown?

How does it grow?

How many different ways is it used?

What other interesting things did you find about the nut?

Information gathered can be illustrated and written down in individual "Research Nutbooks." Display the finished "nutbooks" near the center so that the researched information can be shared.

## 5. YOU'RE A NUT!

**"BARBIE BRAZIL NUT VS. THE NUTCRACKER"**

At one time or another, everyone has had the experience of being called a "nut"—either affectionately or otherwise. Capitalize on this by having children write creative stories, imagining themselves to be real nuts. For example, story starters such as the following create intense interest:

"The Day I Became a Real Nut"

"The Mystery of the Missing Nut"

"The Nut Who Conquered Chicago"

"The Ticklish Nut"

"Wally Walnut Meets Penelope Pecan"

"Peppy Peanut Goes to School"

LEARNING CENTER NO. 22                    Level: GR. 4, 5

## The Time Traveler Center

Curriculum Area:  SOCIAL STUDIES, COLONIAL AMERICA

Goal:  PROMOTING CONCEPTS, CREATIVITY, RESEARCH
SKILLS

Newer trends in social studies have called upon teachers to move from teacher-directed instruction to methods which rely less on memorization of facts and encourage greater student involvement. "Inquiry" and "problem-solving" are two of the terms most widely used to describe these action-oriented processes.

This center was designed to place the children in the role of problem solvers, requiring them to research stimulating questions about life in Colonial times in America. They record the information they uncover and design ways of creatively sharing their findings.

The center should be stocked with a variety of books, maps, photographs, audio-visual aids, and any other learning resources that may aid the students in their investigations.

## GAMES AND ACTIVITIES

### 1. SPY MANUAL

Stock this center with appropriate reference materials about Colonial America. Instruct the children to imagine that they have been placed in a time capsule and taken back in history to the period of Colonial America. In order to report back to their government, they are to keep an accurate account of what happened on their time travels.

The children are to complete the activities that follow.

### A. I'M GOING HERE

In your time capsule there is a map that shows you the way America looked in the 1770s. Write the name of each of the thirteen English colonies on the map.

## B. TAKE A GOOD LOOK

I landed at _____.
This is what I saw:

|   |   |   |   |
|---|---|---|---|
|   |   |   |   |

Choose any place in Colonial America where you imagine your time capsule landed. Draw the first four things that you saw after you emerged from the time capsule.

## C. HEARTY APPETITE

**ALL ABOUT COLONIAL FOOD**

| **LUNCH** | **SUPPER** |
|-----------|------------|
| I HAD: | I HAD: |

In the time it took your time capsule to take you back to the 1770s, you worked up a pretty good appetite. You are eager to see what is available to eat. Where did the food come from? How was it kept from spoiling? In the space above, describe what you found out about food in colonial times. Draw and label what you ate for each meal.

## D. SCHOOL DAZE

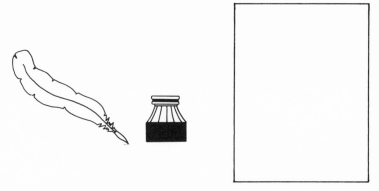

Your journey took you to a Colonial school room. You found that the children didn't have lots of books available. They had to make many of their own books by copying from other books with pen and ink. Show how a typical page written by a Colonial schoolchild looked.

## E. AFTER SCHOOL

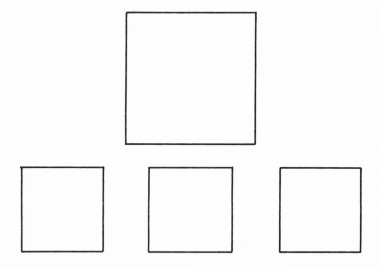

After school, one of the children invited you to visit his home. You discovered that Colonial children had many chores to do when they returned home from school. In the large box, draw a picture of the home you visited. In the three smaller boxes, draw pictures of some of the after-school jobs your new Colonial friend had to do at home.

## F. NEWSPAPER REPORT

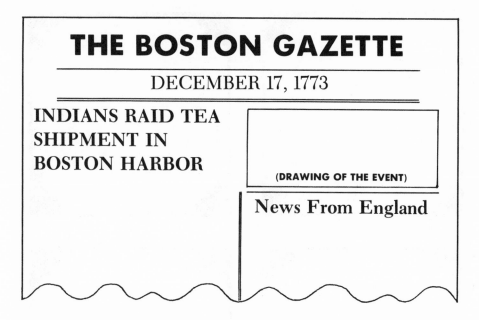

While your friend was doing his chores, he gave you a newspaper to look at. You realized that many important events were occurring in our country at that time. What events did you read about in the newspaper during your time visit? Write the stories that go with the headlines above and draw the picture.

## G. FLAGS

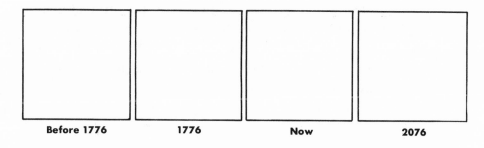

You were surprised to see how different the country's flag looked way back in history. Draw a picture of what the nation's flag looked like at different times in our history. Try to imagine what it might look like in the future.

## H. PHOTO ALBUM

Your friend's father was an important man in Colonial history. Many people came to his house to meet with him.

Draw a picture of the four most unforgettable people you met during your stay. Beneath each picture, describe the work that person was most famous for.

## 2. COLONIAL PARADE

Provide boxes, crepe paper, tagboard, construction paper, clay, and other construction materials. The child is to select a scene, person, object, or event important in Colonial history. She decorates a box with crepe paper and construction paper so that it looks like a parade float. She identifies her selection and constructs, mounts, or draws appropriate items on the box. Arrange the floats in parade fashion near the learning center display.

## 3. COLONIAL HALL OF FAME

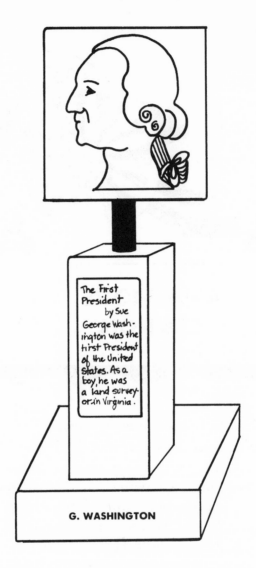

The First
President
        by Sue
George Wash-
ington was the
first President
of the United
States. As a
boy, he was
a land survey-
or in Virginia.

**G. WASHINGTON**

Create pedestals out of boxes mounted on heavy tagboard and display them at the learning center. The children are each to select a person who contributed a great deal to Colonial life. They draw his or her picture, glue a tongue depressor to the back of the picture, and stick it in a pedestal. They write a short description of the chosen person's contributions and paste it on the pedestal below the picture. Add members to the "Hall of Fame" as children contribute their choices.

## 4. COLONIAL TELEVISION

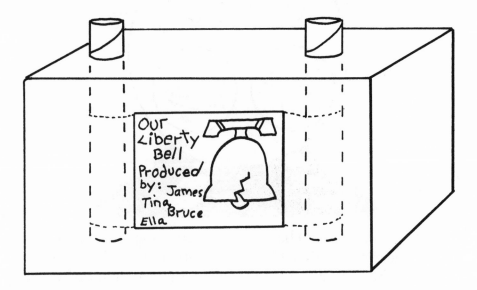

Construct a television box as in the illustration. The children choose an event from Colonial times and work individually or in groups to draw sequential pictures describing the event. They tape their pictures together in a horizontal strip and paste the ends of their story strip onto rollers. They roll the strip so that the title picture shows on the TV screen. They invite other children to the center to enjoy their television presentation.

**5. 2077**

Draw a large crystal ball on construction paper and mount it near the learning center. The children are instructed to imagine what their homes, city, or country will be like one hundred years from now. They write their ideas on circles cut out of construction paper and paste them on the crystal ball.

Questions such as the following can be used to spur their thinking:

What will be the greatest invention?

Where will be the farthest place to which we will travel?

What will your school be like?

What will be the most popular sport?

What kind of transportation will be most popular?

What kinds of jobs will people be doing?

What kinds of foods will people eat?

What will be done to cure hunger? illness? conflict among humans?

LEARNING CENTER NO. 23                    Level: GR. 4 AND UP

## Examining Prefixes and Suffixes

Curriculum Area:  LANGUAGE ARTS, WORD ROOTS, PREFIXES, SUFFIXES

Goal:  PROMOTING SKILLS

Often, learning is directly experiential for young children but becomes largely verbal as children grow older. Upper-grade children enjoy and need action-oriented reinforcement as much as younger children do. At this center, children work at tasks designed to strengthen their understanding of prefixes and suffixes. An important step in developing mature reading and language skills is word analysis. Children need facility in identifying word roots and in recognizing the important changes in meaning that are achieved through affixing. The active experiences at this center not only reinforce these basic skills, but provide the children with opportunities to create interesting individual projects.

## GAMES AND ACTIVITIES

## 1. PREFIX PALETTE

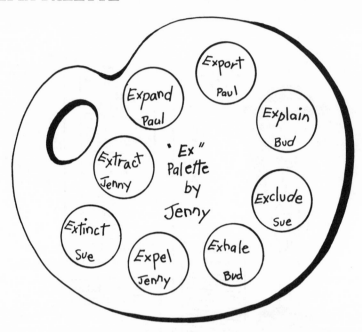

Provide a supply of heavy tagboard palettes, and circles made of construction paper. Three or four children play this game together. One child chooses any prefix listed on the learning center bulletin board and writes the chosen prefix on a palette along with his own name. He takes the dictionary and opens to where words beginning with the chosen prefix are listed. He calls out a definition for one of these words. The first player to identify the word writes it on a construction paper circle, along with her own name, and pastes it on the palette. If no one can guess the word, the player who chose the prefix writes the word on a construction paper circle, along with his own name, and pastes it on the palette. He then calls out another definition. He continues in this way for about five to eight words. Then the second player chooses a different prefix. The game continues in this way until each player has had a turn to choose a prefix. The players add up the number of circles with their names. The highest wins. They may display their palettes in the center area.

## 2. SUFFIX TURTLE

Provide heavy tagboard turtle patterns. Three or four children work together. Each child chooses any suffix from the chart on the learning center board. They each write their chosen suffix and its meaning on a turtle, along with their own names. They pass their turtles around and around, and each child writes a word on the shell of the turtle and signs it. All completed turtles should be displayed in the center area.

## 3. AFFIX RUMMY

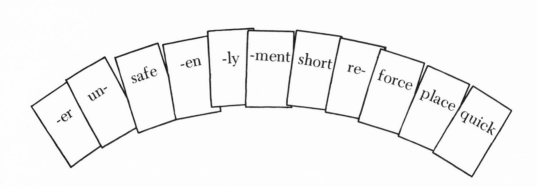

Make a deck of about fifty cards, somewhat as follows:

about eight prefixes in red (some may be repeated)

about eight suffixes in green (some may be repeated)

about thirty-four word roots in black

From two to five children may play. The dealer deals five cards to each player and puts the rest of the deck face down in the middle of the table. The first player draws the top card from the deck. If she has an affix-root word match, she puts it down and the next player draws. If she has no match, she must discard one of her cards face up next to the deck. The next player may take the discard or draw from the top of the pile. Play continues in the same way until someone wins by getting rid of all his cards.

## 4. PREFIX BEE-BOARD

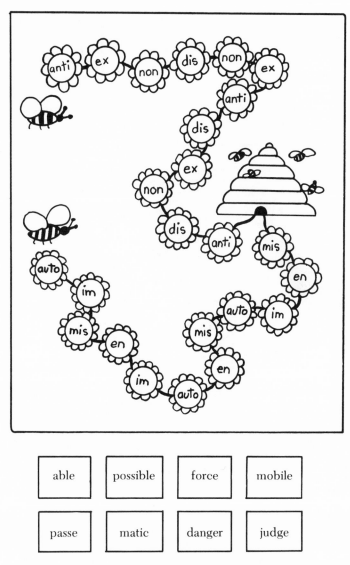

| able | possible | force | mobile |
|------|----------|-------|--------|
| passe | matic | danger | judge |

**WORD ROOT CARDS**

Construct a gameboard as shown, with each flower containing a prefix. Provide colorful bee markers for the players. Make up a deck of cards containing word roots.

Two children play, starting at different ends. The players take turns drawing the top card from the pile. If the word root drawn matches the next prefix, the player may move to that space. If not, he puts the card on the bottom of the deck and waits for his next turn. The first child to the hive is the winner.

## 5. SUFFIX TREASURE BOARD

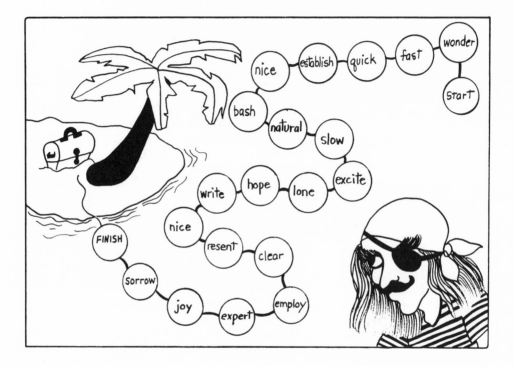

Prepare a gameboard as shown, writing a root word in each space. Make a spinner, writing suffixes in the sections. Provide markers for the players.

The children place their markers on "Start" and take turns spinning the suffix wheel. After spinning, the player examines the gameboard to find the next root word to which that suffix belongs and advances to that space. The first player to reach the treasure is the winner.

LEARNING CENTER NO. 24                    Level: GR. 4 AND UP

## Zilch, Inc. Advertising Your Product

Curriculum Area:  SOCIAL STUDIES, ADVERTISING, LANGUAGE ARTS,
CREATIVE WRITING

Goal:  PROMOTING CREATIVITY, GROWTH IN ATTITUDES
AND VALUES

This center might be used to introduce the study of the purposes, advantages, and disadvantages of advertising media and advertising techniques. It promotes critical attitudes by offering children activities that lead them to analyze their own and their classmates' reactions to commercial attempts to manipulate responses in various ways. The teacher will find that the results and products that emerge from the activities at this center can be very fruitfully followed up with other learning center activities on similar themes and with group discussions and direct teaching.

## GAMES AND ACTIVITIES

## 1. MATCH THE APPEAL

Out of magazines, cut advertisements which reflect different kinds of appeal (as in the illustrations). Mount them on colored construction paper and put them on the learning center background. Beneath each picture, put a box, folder, or envelope. Cut out additional advertisements representing the same approaches and mount them on construction paper. Identify the approach on the back of each advertisement for self-checking, and place them in a box. Have many newspapers and magazines available at the center.

The children take the advertisements out of the box and sort them into the appropriate boxes under the picture. After they check their work, encourage them to search through the newspapers and magazines to find additional advertisements which reflect the appeals described in the center. They can mount them on construction paper, put the answers on the backs, and add them to the box for other students to work at.

## 2. ADVERTISING GIMMICK

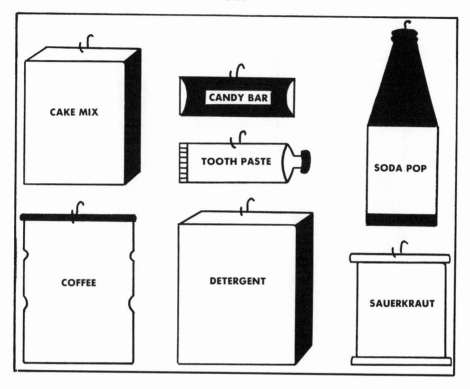

Accumulate some common household products and remove or cover the commercial labels, identifying them simply by content. Stick some drapery hooks through posterboard and hang up the tubes, jars, boxes. The child selects a product and does a promotion job for it. She gives the product a name and writes a convincing ad for it. In writing their ads, the children may use one of the appeals from the previous activity or a new one. Have a supply of drawing paper handy on which children print out and draw the ads for their products.

## 3. GRAPH IT

Provide a stack of magazines at the learning center. Run off copies of a worksheet (as illustrated) to be used by the children in making their surveys. The children should go through the magazines and find contrasting advertisements for one product that is manufactured by two different companies. They mount the two ads on construction paper and show them to a dozen other children in the class. They ask their classmates the questions on the worksheet and graph the results.

## COMPARE WITH CARE
## COLOR A BOX TO SHOW EACH RESPONSE

1. Which ad do you like better?

     COOKA COOLA

     PEEPSI COOLA

2. Which product do you like better?

     COOKA COOLA

     PEEPSI COOLA

3. Which container or package is more appealing?

     COOKA COOLA

     PEEPSI COOLA

4. Which advertising gimmick is more convincing?

     COOKA COOLA

     PEEPSI COOLA

5. Which product would you buy?

     COOKA COOLA

     PEEPSI COOLA

6. My conclusions about advertising as a result of my
    survey are:

_____

_____

_____

## 4. CLASSIFIED SECTION

In this activity, the children advertise a very special product—themselves. Provide paper, crayons, magic markers, magazines, and any other appropriate collage materials. The children are to pretend that they are products to be sold. They are each to draw or find an appropriate picture or illustration, and to think up a phrase or advertising gimmick to guarantee a huge sale. Finished advertisements should be displayed in the learning center area.

LEARNING CENTER NO. 25                    Level: GR. 4 AND UP

# The Solar System Explorers

Curriculum Area:  SCIENCE, LANGUAGE ARTS, PLANETS

Goal:  PROMOTING CONCEPTS, CREATIVITY

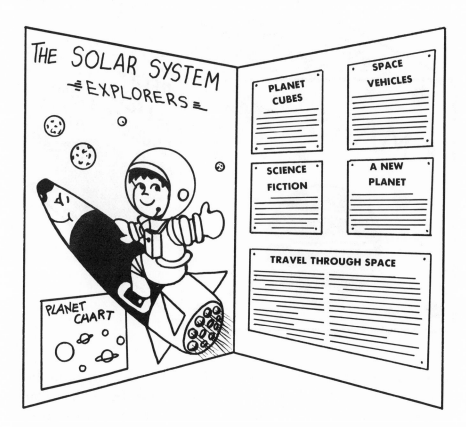

This center serves many purposes as it invites children to search for information about our solar system, present their information in creative ways, and speculate about solutions to unique and imaginary situations. Science skills, social studies skills, language arts skills, and creative arts skills are all interwoven in the pursuit of these projects.

The center should be stocked with a variety of resource materials to aid the children in their investigations. The products that emerge from the children's efforts can be easily arranged into attractive learning center displays.

## GAMES AND ACTIVITIES

### 1. PLANET CUBES

Collect boxes of all shapes and sizes, and place them in the learning center. The child selects any planet from the solar system and uses the books available at the center to research some interesting information about his chosen planet. He selects a box and decorates all six sides to depict the facts he has discovered.

## 2. SPACE VEHICLES

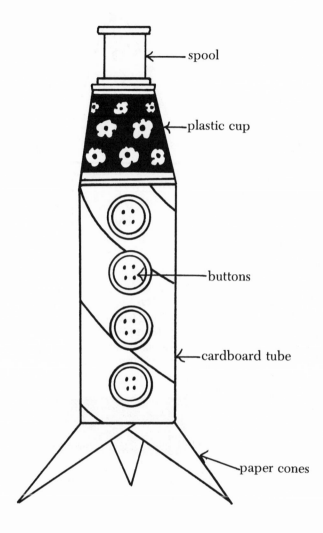

spool

plastic cup

buttons

cardboard tube

paper cones

Provide a variety of materials which can be used in construction, such as, cardboard tubes, paper cups, paint, straws, plastic lids, small boxes, wire hangers, spools, buttons, paper plates, bags, and so on. The children are to use the materials to design space vehicles of the year 2077. Display their creations on a table near the learning center.

## 3. TRAVEL THROUGH SPACE

My Trip To
PLUTO
by
Florence

We reached Pluto at 3:00. It was very cold and there was a clear black sky. No one lives there because there is no air or water. We found many rocks.

Instruct the children to pretend they are space explorers in the year 3000. Provide rocket-shaped worksheets.

The children are to take an imaginary journey to any planet on the solar system chart. Have them use the rocket-shaped worksheet paper to keep a log of their trip. They are to record times of take-off and landing, events, mishaps, observations, before and after landing.

## 4. A NEW PLANET

Provide a variety of art materials. Instruct the children to each use the materials to draw a picture or construct a collage of a new planet which they discovered on an imaginary trip through space. The children should invent names for their new planets. They may write about their planets if they wish. Display their work near the learning center on a bulletin board labeled "The Mystery Planet."

## 5. SCIENCE FICTION

The children each make up a science adventure about an unknown space vehicle crash landing on earth. They illustrate their stories and display their books near the center. The class can choose the best story and turn it into a TV film or a play to dramatize and present to an invited audience.

LEARNING CENTER NO. 26                    Level: GR. 5

# Map Detectives

Curriculum Area:  SOCIAL STUDIES, MAP READING
Goal:  PROMOTING SKILLS, CONCEPTS

The activities at this center require that children have some familiarity with map reading and know directions. Now they have varied opportunities to practice these skills in practical ways. They use maps and graphs to complete and compete in these activities. Games may be played over and over, giving needed drill, while motivation remains high. The center should be stocked with atlases, maps, and globes that the children may use for checking and reference purposes.

## GAMES AND ACTIVITIES

## 1. RESCUE MISSION

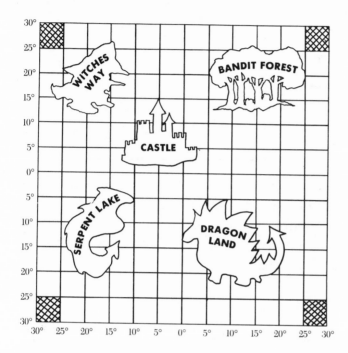

Construct a large game board, graph paper style, as in the illustration. Each square represents five degrees. The castle is in the center of the board, and four danger zones are marked off in irregular patterns in different areas of the board. Provide markers of four different colors. Make a spinner with nine sections. Mark eight of these sections as follows: 5°N, 10°N, 5°E, 10°E, 5°S, 10°S, 5°W, 10°W. Mark one section ZONK.

The object of the game is to reach the castle to free the princess who is imprisoned there. Four players may use this game. Each player places her marker at one of the four corners. Taking turns, they spin the spinner, which tells how far (in degrees) and in which direction to move. If the player will land in a clear space, she may make the move. However, if a player will land in a danger zone (Dragon Land, Serpent Lake, etc.), she may not make the move, but remains where she was until her next turn. If the player spins to ZONK, she must go back to her corner and start all over again. The first player to reach the castle is the winner.

## 2. TRAVEL WITH THE STARS

| BASEBALL SCHEDULE TAMPA PALMETTOS | |
|---|---|
| July 15 | Atlanta Squirrels |
| July 23 | Cleveland Larks |
| Aug. 4 | Newark Stars |
| Aug. 14 | Chicago Hares |
| Aug. 22 | Omaha Stallions |
| Aug. 28 | Carson City Crowns |

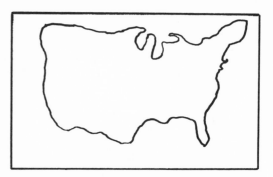

For this activity, prepare dittoes of an outline map of the United States. Get (or make up) the schedules of several major professional sports teams. Copy these on tagboard and mount them at the center. Prepare a second ditto with questions for the students to answer, such as:

1. What is your team's home town?

2. What is the farthest city to which your team must travel?

3. Which of the teams your team is playing is located farthest west? north? east? south?

4. Of all the cities your team will play in, which are larger than your team's home town? which are smaller? about the same size?

5. How many miles will your team travel all together to complete all the games?

The child is to choose her favorite team and, using the outline map, mark the path the team will follow in order to complete all of the games on its schedule. She is to put No. 1 on the first city, No. 2 on the next, and so on. She is also to indicate on the map the number of miles the team will travel between each stop. Then the child is to answer the questions on the second ditto. When she has finished, she can find someone in the class who chose the same team and they can compare their work, checking each other out.

## 3. MAPS BY CODE

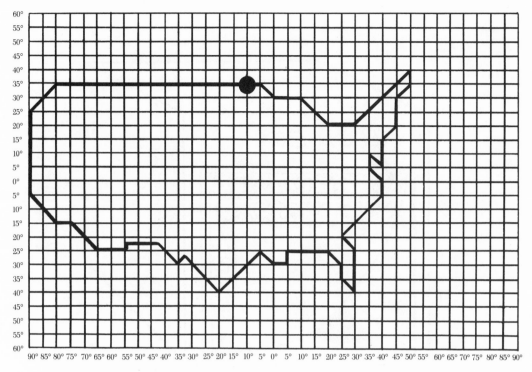

**MAP A    THE COUNTRY IS** _____

Prepare graph dittoes marked off from a central axis in five-degree boxes. Put a starting dot in the corner of one box. Prepare sets of directions which will create a rough outline of some country, as in the example illustrated below:

| | | | | |
|---|---|---|---|---|
| a. 5°E | i. 10°S | q. 5°SE | y. 5°NW | gg. 10°NW |
| b. 5°SE | j. 5°SW | r. 15°S | z. 15°SW | hh. 5°W |
| c. 10°E | k. 10°S | s. 5°NW | aa. 12½°NW | ii. 10°NW |
| d. 10°SE | l. 5°NW | t. 5°N | bb. 2½°SW | jj. 30°N |
| e. 10°E | m. 5°S | u. 5°NW | cc. 7½°NW | kk. 10°NE |
| f. 20°NE | n. 5°SE | v. 15°W | dd. 12½°W | ll. 70°E |
| g. 5°S | o. 5°S | w. 5°S | ee. 2½°S | |
| h. 5°SW | p. 15°SW | x. 5°W | ff. 10°W | |

Several sets of directions can be prepared outlining different countries. The student takes a graph paper ditto and follows the directions that go with that ditto. Starting at the dot, he makes dots at each successive point designated in the directions. Then he connects all the dots and identifies the country.

## 4. MYSTERY LAND

Make a cardboard outline of a state, country, or continent and put it inside a "Feely Box." The children are to reach into the box and, by touch alone, they are to identify the mystery land. When they think they have guessed what it is, they find it on the map. Then they take the outline out of the box and compare it with the map to see if they were right.

Put a new outline in the box every few days.

## 5. BATTLEGROUND

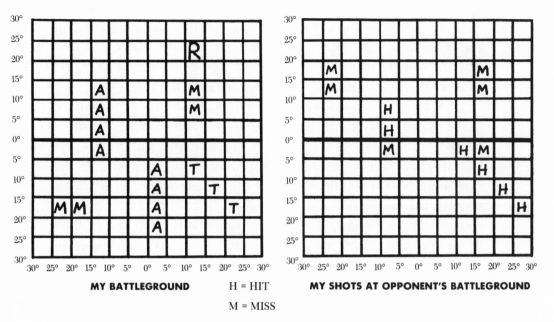

**MY BATTLEGROUND**  H = HIT  **MY SHOTS AT OPPONENT'S BATTLEGROUND**

M = MISS

Prepare four large tagboard playing boards, two for each player. Each board is divided into a grid pattern with the rows and columns numbered so that they represent degrees of latitude and longitude. Laminate the boards so that players may write on them and erase what they have written when they are finished with the game, leaving the boards for the next players.

In this game, each player has the following armaments:

two artillery guns, each taking up four squares (AAAA   AAAA)

one tank taking up three squares (TTT)

two mortar guns, each taking up two squares (MM   MM)

one rifle taking up one square (R)

The object of the game is to destroy the opponent's gun placements before your own are wiped out.

Each holding one board so that it cannot be seen by the other player, the players deploy their armaments anywhere they want to on the board by writing the appropriate initials in the squares. They may choose horizontal, vertical, or diagonal patterns, but different gun types must not touch each other. The other two boards will be used to record each player's shots so that the players can try to locate the opponent's patterns.

Players take turns shooting in rounds. Each player may shoot at the opponent five consecutive times in each round. A "shot" is taken by identifying a square by latitude and longitude—for example, 20° W, 10° S. The first player calls the shot and the opponent tells whether a hit or a miss was scored. The player records this information on his second board and calls the next shot. After five shots, it is the opponent's turn to shoot. The rounds continue until one player has hit all of the opponent's gun squares.

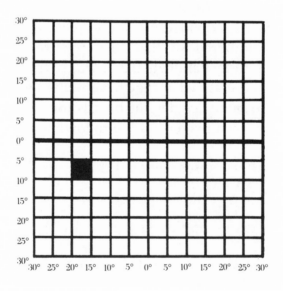

LEARNING CENTER NO. 27                              Level: GR. 5

## Parts of Speech Are Important

Curriculum Area:  LANGUAGE, PARTS OF SPEECH

Goal:  PROMOTING SKILLS

Elementary school children frequently express greater dis-pleasure with being required to memorize the parts of speech than with any other task in the language arts. Yet, teachers persist in using this approach in teaching grammatic concepts. Children need a greater variety of more highly motivating activities if the concepts are really to become meaningful to them. This center offers a variety of enjoyable and challenging individual and group activities to insure interest in learning. The exercises call upon children to reinforce and extend their understandings of the parts of speech in a meaningful and delightful way. Often humor, especially in the form of incongruity, is the best spur to memory.

## GAMES AND ACTIVITIES

## 1. HEADLINE NEWS

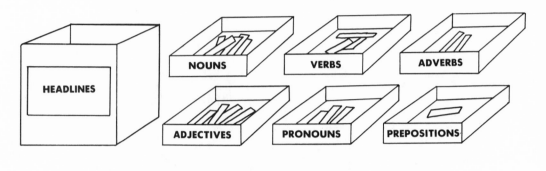

| WHALE BEACHED <u>YESTERDAY</u> |

| <u>LARGE</u> CROWD AT CHAMPIONSHIP GAME |

Select headlines from major stories in the newspaper. Cut them out and mount them on heavy tagboard strips. Underline one word in each headline. Be sure that the various parts of speech are represented among the underlined words. Write the answers on the backs of the strips, or use symbols on the boxes and on the backs of the strips. Place all the headlines in a large box. Provide boxes, each labeled with a part of speech.

The children are to sort all the headlines into the boxes in which the underlined words belong. They check their own work.

## 2. GRAB!

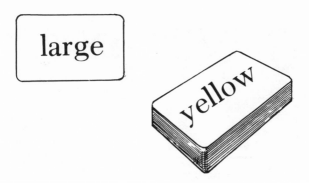

Prepare a set of about fifty cards by writing a different word on each card. Be sure that you have included an equal number of each part of speech, for example, fourteen nouns, fourteen verbs fourteen adjectives, fourteen pronouns.

Two children play this game. The dealer deals out the whole deck, one card at a time, face down in two piles. Then the players simultaneously turn over the top cards of their piles. If the two cards do not belong to the same part of speech, both players turn over the second cards, then the third cards, etc. If, at any point, both players turn up cards that are the same part of speech, they must call out the part of speech. The player who notices that the cards match and calls the name of the category (e.g., "Nouns!") wins all the cards that are already turned up. These cards are placed face down at the bottom of this player's pile. The play continues until one player "grabs" all the cards.

## 3. LISTEN AND TELL

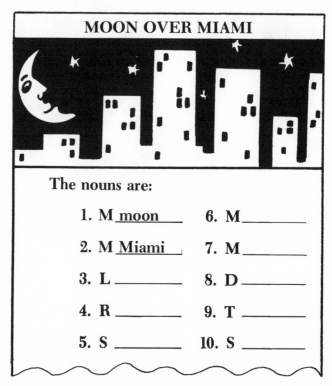

MOON OVER MIAMI

The nouns are:

1. M _moon_          6. M _____

2. M _Miami_         7. M _____

3. L _____         8. D _____

4. R _____         9. T _____

5. S _____        10. S _____

Tape record several popular songs. A separate song can be used for practice with each part of speech being developed—noun, verb, adjective, etc.

Prepare a worksheet similar to the one illustrated, indicating the number of words to listen for in the specific category and providing first-letter clues in sequence. You should attempt to spread your word clues out so that the listener can function at a comfortable level. Provide an answer key.

The children are to listen carefully to the record and try to pick out the words which function as the identified part of speech. They check their own work.

## 4. MY WORD!

> "_____!" he shouted, _____,
> (*exclamation*)                (*adverb*)
>
> as he ran down the _____and
>                    (*noun*)
>
> kissed his _____ wife good-bye.
>            (*adjective*)
>
> "I'm late for _____ again," he
>               (*noun*)
>
> muttered as he jumped into his _____
>                                (*adjective*)
>
> _____ and drove hurriedly away.
> (*noun*)
>
> What a perfectly _____
>                  (*adjective*)
>
> day in the _____ household.
>            (*proper noun*)

Write some short stories, leaving blank spaces at various points and indicating what part of speech is to go in the blank. Illustrate the stories. Laminate them so they may be reused.

Two or more children may play this game. One child acts as Reader and the other(s) as Writer(s). The Reader selects one of the stories and, without showing it to the others, asks each Writer, in turn, to give a part of speech ("adjective," etc.) called for in the story. The Reader writes those words in the blank spaces in the story. When all the spaces are filled, the Reader reads the story back to the Writers. If they think their story is very funny, they may copy it on a piece of paper. Later, a contest may be held with the whole class choosing the most outrageous version of each story.

LEARNING CENTER NO. 28                     Level: GR. 5

## Metric Measures . . . A Real Blast!!

Curriculum Area:   MATH, METRIC MEASUREMENTS

Goal:   PROMOTING SKILLS

The metric system is gradually making its way into all of our lives. Newspapers, grocery store packaging, weather reports, and many other materials we encounter in our daily experiences bring the metric system to us. At one time or another, we have all struggled to understand this unfamiliar system of measurement. Children, too, face many of the same predicaments. In order to assist them in understanding this new concept in measurement, learning experiences should be made as concrete as possible.

This center was designed to provide concrete but interesting experiences. Children are encouraged to measure, weigh, estimate, and predict metric data in a variety of hands-on encounters. Through group and individual activities, children are encouraged to be creative as well as to master the metric system.

**GAMES AND ACTIVITIES**

## 1. SORT 'EM OUT

Provide small sorting boxes, each labeled for a different category of measurement. Make each box a different color.

Prepare a set of cards, drawing or pasting pictures of various common objects on each card and indicating the metric measurement of each object. On the back of each card, paste a colored square indicating the measurement category.

The children sort the cards into the boxes they think they belong in. They check their work by seeing if the color code on the back of the card matches the color of the sorting box.

## 2. METRIC WAR

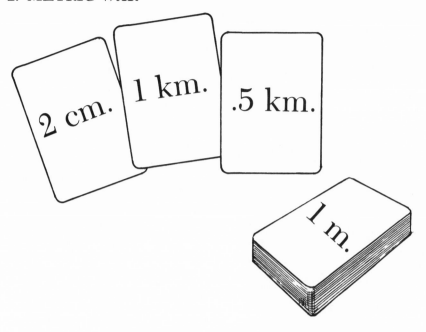

Prepare several decks of small cards, each deck containing a different set of metric measurements, for example, one set for volume, another for weight, another for length, and another for area. Each deck may be distinguished by a different color. Each game is played for a specified time (designated by the teacher, or decided upon by the children, as you prefer).

The children choose one of the decks. The dealer shuffles the cards and deals out all cards in turn to the players. Simultaneously, each player turns the top card face up. The child whose metric measure is largest claims all the turned up cards. At the end of the designated time period, the child with the largest number of cards wins. The children may then choose another deck with a different measure.

## 3. WE GROW UP

| Name | Length at Birth | Present Height | How Much I Grew | How Tall I Will Get | Weight at Birth | Present Weight | How Much I Gained | How Much I Will Weigh at 25 |
|---|---|---|---|---|---|---|---|---|
| Juan | | | | | | | | |
| Katrina | | | | | | | | |
| Libby | | | | | | | | |
| Jan | | | | | | | | |
| Ray | | | | | | | | |
| Tony | | | | | | | | |
| Maurice | | | | | | | | |
| Clovice | | | | | | | | |
| Lars | | | | | | | | |
| Mitchell | | | | | | | | |
| Lee | | | | | | | | |

Mount a large class chart, like the one illustrated, at the learning center. Encourage the children to bring in information from home regarding their weight and length at birth, and to record these data in metric measurements on the chart. Instruct them to use the meter stick to measure their present height. They weigh themselves on the scale and record their present weight in metric measurement. The children should find it interesting to predict the height and weight they will achieve as adults.

## 4. GUESS-TIMATE BOX

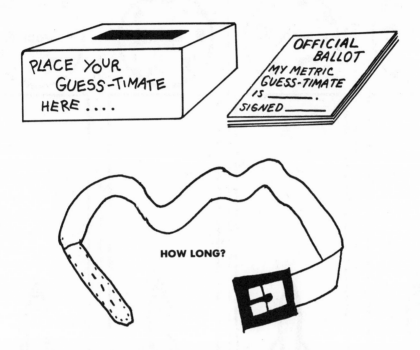

Place a common object—such as an envelope, a box, a can—on display in the learning center. Instruct children to estimate its metric measure. Change the display periodically. Use different measurements at different times, such as the length of a piece of chalk, the area of a sheet of construction paper, the volume of water held by a drinking glass, the weight of a book, etc.

Provide ballots on which the children write their estimates and a Voting Box into which they put their ballots. The child whose estimate comes the closest to the actual metric measurement is designated the "Metric Champ" for that period. Place a picture of the "Metric Champ" on the learning center display.

## 5. BLAST OFF

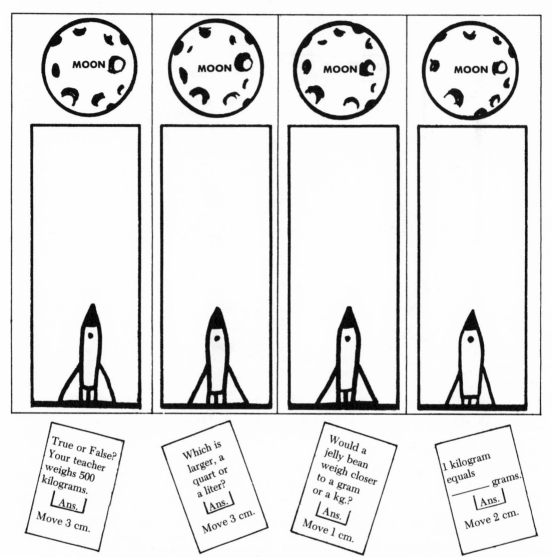

True or False?
Your teacher
weighs 500
kilograms.
⌊Ans.⌋
Move 3 cm.

Which is
larger, a
quart or
a liter?
⌊Ans.⌋
Move 3 cm.

Would a
jelly bean
weigh closer
to a gram
or a kg.?
⌊Ans.⌋
Move 1 cm.

1 kilogram
equals
____ grams.
⌊Ans.⌋
Move 2 cm.

Prepare a game board as illustrated, and a deck of cards containing questions for metric review. Write the answers under tabs.

Four children can play this game at one time. The children, in turn, select a card from the top of the pile. If the child answers the question correctly, she uses the metric ruler to move her rocket the distance specified on the question card. If she is incorrect, the rocket must stay where it is. The first player to reach the moon is the winner.

## 6. MORRIS THE METRIC MONSTER!

Prepare story sheets, such as the ones illustrated, about an imaginary creature. The children complete the stories by estimating various metric measurements proportionate for the creature's size.

---

**MORRIS THE METRIC MONSTER**

Morris is a giant-sized monster. He is _____ tall and weighs _____. His arms are about _____ long. He must wear size _____ shoes in order to fit his _____ long feet. When he takes one step with his long legs he covers a length of _____.

Imagine a person that big in real life! It must cost a fortune just to give Morris three square meals a day. Below is a list of foods which a normal person might use in a week. Fill out the shopping list to show how much food you'd have to buy to feed Morris each week.

---

| NORMAL PERSON | MORRIS |
|---|---|
| 1/2 kilogram of jelly beans | |
| 2 kilogram bag of apples | |
| 3 kilograms of chicken | |
| 200 grams of cereal | |
| 5 liters of milk | |
| 454 grams of butter | |
| 3.8 liters of ice cream | |

Scale:   1 cm. = __20__ m.

BEDROOM (40M x 30M)    DEN    GAME ROOM

HOME SWEET HOME

LIVING ROOM (45M x 30M)    KITCHEN (50M x 40M)

BATHROOM

### MORRIS'S HOUSE

Imagine Morris coming home after a hard day's work! Squeek! Creak! Kapow! . . . Morris opens the door and enters his living room. Make a scale drawing of how you think his house looks. Choose how many meters will be represented by one centimeter on your map. Then draw all the rooms in the house to scale. Record the dimensions of Morris's bedroom, living room, kitchen on your map.

LEARNING CENTER NO. 29                                    Level: GR. 5

## Building New Fraction Skills

Curriculum Area:   MATH, FRACTIONS

Goal: PROMOTING SKILLS

It is quite common for children to experience great difficulty in understanding fractions, especially if the only learning experiences to which they have been exposed involve textbook assignments. This center actively engages children in activities that involve the use of fractions in a variety of meaningful situations. By providing highly motivating learning opportunities for children in an area that is traditionally drab and difficult, the center happily reinforces skills and concepts.

## GAMES AND ACTIVITIES

### 1. EQUIVALENTS BOARD

Construct a triangular stand, approximately 12″ x 5″, as shown. Prepare three sets of cards—one set with fractions written in numerals, one set with illustrations for the fractions used, and one set with the fractions written out in words. On the back of each card, use a picture, letter, or number symbol for matching sets. Using large rings, attach the cards to the stand so that each card may be flipped over.

The children flip over the cards until they get a set of three that match. They check their own work by looking at the backs of the cards to see if they are all marked with the same symbol.

## 2. FRACTION ORDER

Make a set of about fifty-two cards, each containing a different fraction. Several children may play this game together. One child acts as the caller. The caller shuffles the cards and deals out three cards face down to each player. On the caller's signal, "Go," all the players turn over their cards and arrange them in sequence from small to large. The first person to complete the task correctly wins one point. A person who declares to be a winner but displays the wrong sequence loses one point. The first player to get ten points is the winner.

## 3. FRACTION WAR

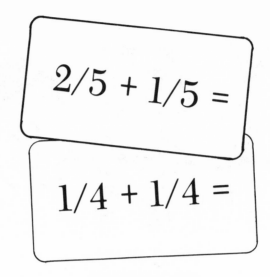

**FRACTION WAR CARDS**

Make a set of fifty-two cards, each card containing an addition, subtraction, multiplication, or division problem involving fractions.

Two to four children may play together. One child deals out all the cards face down, to the players. Simultaneously, all the players take their top card, turn it over, and work the problem shown. The player whose answer is the largest wins all the turned up cards. The play continues in this way, with all the players turning over their top cards at the same time and the highest number winning all the open cards. The teacher will be consulted in case of any disagreement. The game is over when a player has won all the cards; or a time for play may be designated and the winner is the one with the most cards at the end of the specified time.

## 4. FRACTION BATTLEFIELD

| | | |
|:---:|:---:|:---:|
| $\frac{1}{18}$ | $\frac{2}{18}$ | $\frac{3}{18}$ |
| $\frac{4}{18}$ | $\frac{5}{18}$ | $\frac{6}{18}$ |
| $\frac{7}{18}$ | $\frac{8}{18}$ | $\frac{9}{18}$ |
| $\frac{10}{18}$ | $\frac{11}{18}$ | $\frac{12}{18}$ |
| $\frac{13}{18}$ | $\frac{14}{18}$ | $\frac{15}{18}$ |
| $\frac{16}{18}$ | $\frac{17}{18}$ | $\frac{18}{18}$ |

**BATTLE BOARD**

Prepare a gameboard for a specific fraction, as illustrated. Using foam rubber cubes, make three dice. Write a different fraction on each side. Prepare colored markers by cutting squares out of construction paper.

Two or three children may play this game. Each chooses a different colored marker. The children take turns rolling all three dice. The roller selects any *one* of the three fractions rolled and places a marker on the gameboard square which corresponds to the chosen die. The children keep rolling in turn until all of the spaces on the board have been covered. The winner is the player who has the most markers on the board.

LEARNING CENTER NO. 30                          Level: GR. 5—7

## Come See the Magnetic Attractions

Curriculum Area:  SCIENCE, MAGNETS

Goal:  DEVELOPING CONCEPTS

The children will use a variety of materials to discover some properties of magnetism. They will pursue scientific procedures like all good scientists, experimenting with materials, observing the results, and recording the information they uncover. They will also use reference sources to check their hypotheses and conclusions.

For each activity, the students get a worksheet. They follow the directions given for procedures in conducting the experiment and record their observations on the worksheet. In addition, each activity has a "Thought Challenge" which invites the students to apply their observed results in seeking underlying concepts and relationships.

## GAMES AND ACTIVITIES

## 1. WHAT IS A MAGNET?

Provide a plastic bag filled with sawdust shavings. Put a magnet and some nails, tacks, buttons, pebbles, and pins in a box. Give the children worksheets with the following directions:

Pour some of the sawdust out on a desk.

Scatter some of the objects throughout the sawdust.

Move the magnet through the mixture and observe what happens.

Record your observations on this paper.

They then answer the following *Thought Challenge:*

> Put a paper clip in a glass of water and then try to take it out without getting your fingers wet! How did you do it?

## 2. WHAT WILL A MAGNET ATTRACT?

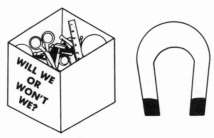

Put many objects into a box labeled "Will We or Won't We?" Include many objects made of iron or steel, as well as some made of wood, rubber, plastic, tin, silver, gold. Provide a magnet and copies of the worksheet (like the one below) on which students record their findings. Direct students to place each object on the table, touch the magnet to the object, and record their results on the worksheet.

| My magnet attracted these objects: | My magnet did not attract these objects: |
| --- | --- |
| | |

Conclusion: Objects made of _____ and _____ will be attracted by a magnet.

They then use the reference books you have stocked the center with to answer the following *Thought Challenge:*

> Why do magnets attract objects which contain only iron or steel?
>
> How can you test a metal to find out whether it contains iron or steel?

They put their answers into a folder to be checked by the teacher.

## 3. MAKE A MAGNET

Provide many small objects made of metal, such as steel nails, keys, knives. Also provide many thumb tacks, a hammer, and copies of a worksheet, as illustrated below.

Instruct the student to magnetize a steel nail by rubbing it in only one direction with a strong magnet until the nail can pick up a thumb tack. Then the student is to rub the nail ten more times and see if it will pick up more tacks. The student is to try making the nail magnet stronger and stronger, recording the results on the worksheet. Then the student tries to make a magnet using at least two other metal objects and following the same procedure.

| No. of times I rubbed | No. of thumb tacks the nail magnet picked up | No. of thumb tacks the _____ picked up | No. of thumb tacks the _____ picked up |
|:---:|:---:|:---:|:---:|
| 10 | | | |
| 20 | | | |
| 30 | | | |
| 40 | | | |
| 50 | | | |
| Which metal objects became magnetized? | | | |

The student then tries the following *Thought Challenge:*

Hit your magnetized nail sharply with a hammer. What happened to its magnetism? Look through the reference materials to find the explanation.

## 4. MAKE A MAGNET WITH ELECTRICITY

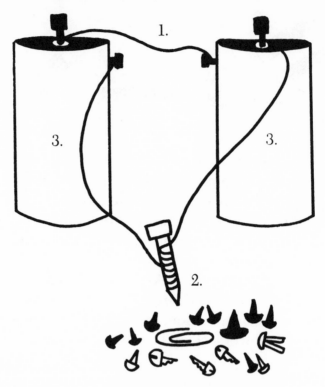

Provide batteries and electrical wire so that students can make and experiment with electric magnets. Instruct the students as follows:

1. Cut a short piece of wire and remove about an inch of insulation from both ends of the wire. Connect one end to the center terminal of one battery and the other end to the outside terminal of the other battery.

2. Take a long piece of wire and, working from the middle of the wire, wind ten wraps around a heavy nail, leaving about one foot of free wire hanging from each side of the nail.

3. Remove about an inch of insulation from both ends of the wire and connect one end to the center terminal of one battery and the other end to the outside terminal of the other battery.

Having closed the electric circuit, the student is to experiment by holding the wired nail close to various metal objects, such as nails, pins, tacks, paper fasteners, and screws. The student observes what happened.

The student then tries the following *Thought Challenge*:

> Vary the number of wraps around the nail and record on the worksheet the number of objects picked up each time.

| Number of Wraps | Objects picked up |
|---|---|
| 10 | |
| 15 | |
| 20 | |
| 25 | |
| 30 | |
| Does increasing the number of wraps around the nail strengthen the magnet? Why? | |

## 5. MAGNETIC BOAT RACE

Provide all the materials (corks, clips, pins, dowels, magnets, pan) and directions for students to make boats and to have a race by using magnets. Two students work together, each making a boat using the following directions:

1. Bend up one end of a paper clip and stick it into a cork.

2. Stick a pin into the other side of the cork.

3. Cut a triangle out of colored paper and paste it to the pin to make a sail.

4. Take a wooden dowel and tape a small magnet firmly to the end.

Now the students fill a pan with water and suspend the pan across two piles of blocks, making sure the pan is level. They float their boats in the water, manuevering them from below with the magnetic rods.

Each student tries to answer the following *Thought Challenge*:

Can you think of some ways to make your boat faster or your opponent's boat slower?

# SECTION 3

# ORGANIZING AND MANAGING
# AN INDIVIDUALIZED
# OPEN-CONCEPT CLASSROOM

## Making the Changeover

SLOW AND STEADY WINS THE RACE

The major key to a successful start in using the learning center approach is thoughtful and deliberate planning. Introducing this innovation all at once by setting up several centers and expecting each child to work independently at them may bring the same results the hare experienced in the race with the tortoise. Because of the novel situation in which they find themselves, the children will be enthusiastic and all too willing to rush headlong into their new experience. However, if you have introduced the learning center approach precipitously, you will find that the children do not really understand learning centers and what they should do with them. This predicament may unfortunately result in a total collapse of classroom confidence and create a negative feeling toward the approach. At this point, you realize that your children needed a more careful introduction to guide them in crossing the bridge between the formal classroom environment and the new learning center environment.

In introducing learning centers, it is best to follow the tortoise's gait rather than the hare's, establishing a starting point and proceeding very slowly while clearly explaining every step along the way to the children. Gradually, you will find that your classroom is operating smoothly and efficiently, without the pitfalls and setbacks that befall the teacher who is impulsive and hasty.

The following are suggestions for gradually introducing the learning center approach into your classroom:

1. Start with one or two reinforcement learning centers designed to be used in conjunction with some current classroom work. In this way, the children will not view the learning center activities as extra frills in the school day, but will sense their relationship and valuable contribution to the school program. Reading and math are two areas of the school curriculum which are especially adaptable to this gradual approach. The chart that follows illustrates one teacher's plan for introducing reinforcement learning centers into the classroom.

In this example, while the teacher is working with one reading group in a basic reading activity, another group is doing related seatwork, while the third group is engaged in independent learning center work created by the teacher to reinforce the skills worked upon in the reading lesson. At specific time intervals, the children move to new areas to pursue new learning activities.

|  | 9:00 - 9:20 | 9:20 - 9:40 | 9:40 - 10:00 |
|---|---|---|---|
| GROUP 1 | Group work with teacher (Read from basal) | Follow-up activities (Workbook) | Center time |
| GROUP 2 | Follow-up activities (Workbook) | Center time | Group work with teacher (Read from basal) |
| GROUP 3 | Center time | Group work with teacher (Read from basal) | Follow-up activities (Workbook) |

2. Gradually, you may wish to increase the amount of time the children spend working with the learning centers. There are various ways of doing this. The plans that follow illustrate two different methods.

In the Daily Plan, the teacher decided that in addition to providing reinforcement centers for some children in some areas of curriculum, one hour of the regular school day was to be set aside for learning center activities for all children. In this way, opportunities are provided for all children to benefit from the use of centers. This avoids the trap that may be inherent in using centers as a supplement to regular subject area classroom work of having such centers become a reward for those children who complete their regular assignments before other children.

One word of caution about allotting a daily time slot for the use of centers—never use the last period of the day for such activity. Reserving the end of the day for independent and active learning may lead the children to believe that center time is merely a "fun and play" period which really doesn't contribute much to the regular learning routine in the classroom. Choose a time slot during the day which is convenient and provides continuity with the rest of the school program.

| DAILY PLAN | | | | | |
|---|---|---|---|---|---|
| 9:00 - 10:00 | 10:00 - 10:30 | 11:00 - 11:45 | 1:00 - 2:00 | 2:00 - 2:15 | 2:30 - 3:00 |
| *READING*<br><br>Group 1<br><br>Basal readers. Discuss story. Workbook page 53.<br><br><br>Group 2<br><br>Workbook pages 71-73. Centers when finished.<br><br><br>Group 3<br><br>Learning Centers. Basal reader page 94. | *SOCIAL STUDIES*<br><br><br>All children work on special projects | *MATH*<br><br>Group 1<br><br>Addition and subtraction problems—p. 44. Centers when finished.<br><br><br>Group 2<br><br>Chalkboard game with teacher. Page 32 in math book when finished. | Learning Centers for all children | *DISCUSSION*<br><br><br>Informally discuss the reactions of the children to their learning center experiences | *LANGUAGE ARTS*<br><br>Creative writing— Haiku poems. |

In the Weekly Plan, the teacher sets aside one day during the week when the children work exclusively in learning centers. This implies that the centers can achieve essentially the same goals as the normal program; and in addition, centers provide opportunities for making choices and pursuing individual interests while building skills, concepts, and attitudes.

| WEEKLY PLAN | | | | |
|---|---|---|---|---|
| **Monday** | **Tuesday** | **Wednesday** | **Thursday** | **Friday** |
| Regular Program | Regular Program | Regular Program | Learning Center Day | Regular Program |

3. The rate at which you may further extend the use of learning centers will become readily apparent by the time you have followed some of these gradual procedures. By thoroughly evaluating the capabilities of your children in working with the centers, as well as observing their desire to·work in such a new classroom environment, you will begin to sense the amount of guidance necessary to move toward a complete decentralized approach to classroom instruction.

When you have begun to introduce new centers and to decentralize the surroundings, adequate space may pose a formidable problem. Grouping desks may alleviate this problem and help you move to a less formal classroom setting.

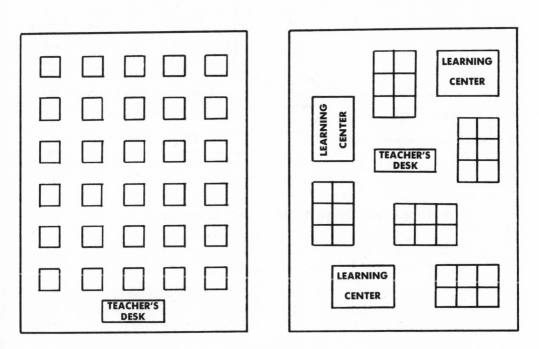

The transition from the formal arrangement of rows of desks to functional groupings of materials and equipment can be achieved in stages. Gradually, your room may evolve into an environment which encourages the children to experience more and more physical and academic freedom. By removing some student desks, grouping others, bringing in tables, placing bookcases and screens where they serve as partitions, introducing a couch or pillows in a reading corner, and so on, the classroom atmosphere changes from a formalized environment to an informal activity-oriented place where children experience opportunities for working independently, by themselves or in small groups.

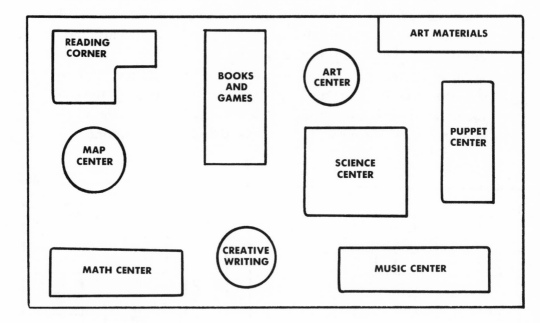

## Planning and Organizing the Routines

The way you organize your classroom often affects the extent to which the children will become absorbed in the learning center activities. It also determines the effectiveness of classroom management. The following suggestions should be considered:

1. Separate areas which involve quiet activities from those which involve noisy activity.

2. Provide areas for individual work as well as areas for group interaction.

3. Reserve areas for the purpose of displaying the children's work.

4. Make provisions for neat storage of supplies and materials.

5. Arrange for adequate procedures in moving your pupils
   to and from learning centers.

The method of movement you decide upon will closely
reflect your personal educational philosophy, which will probably follow one of these patterns:

| | |
|---|---|
| Pattern 1 | Teacher makes all learning center assign-ments. |
| Pattern 2 | Teacher provides child with two or three alternatives and the child chooses from among them. |
| Pattern 3 | Teacher and children choose jointly from among all possible choices. |
| Pattern 4 | Children have free choice of all learning possibilities. Teacher serves as a source for verification, classification, and evaluation. |

Among the scheduling procedures you may wish to consider
are: concrete techniques, charts, contracts.

## A. Concrete Techniques

For young children, planning guides should be as concrete as
possible. This helps them to understand what they are to do in
the various centers. Having a concrete, visual plan also helps
children use their working time appropriately. Several concrete
planning devices follow.

*Pictures*

Mount close-up photographs or self-portraits of each child on tagboard cards and glue a clothespin to each card. A large tagboard sign depicts the various learning center areas. The pictures of the children are clipped to sections of this sign to indicate the centers they are to work in. The pictures may be moved when the children change centers.

*Necklaces*

Draw and cut out symbols to represent each learning center activity. String yarn or ribbon through the symbol, making a necklace. Make a number of necklaces for each center according to the number of children you wish to work there. Place the appropriate necklaces around the children's necks to indicate which center they are to use during a specific period.

*Wheels*

Make a tagboard wheel with a picture of each learning center in each section. Print each child's name on a clothespin. Clip the clothespins to the sections of the wheel to indicate the centers at which the children will work.

Make a large wheel from a sheet of heavy tagboard. Print the names of the children's work groups around the outer rim of the wheel. Prepare a smaller wheel; draw pictures and print the names of the learning center areas in each section. The wheel may be turned to indicate the center to which each group is assigned.

*Tickets*

Color code your centers. Use construction paper in corresponding colors to make tickets for admission to each center.

Give out the appropriate number of tickets of each color to the children who are to work at each center. The children match the color of their tickets to the color symbol at the learning center.

*Boxes*

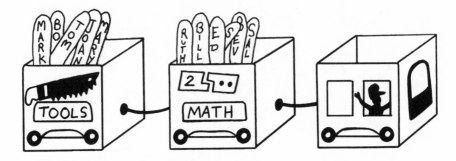

Decorate a series of small boxes to indicate the names of the activities in the learning centers. String them together box-car fashion. Print each child's name on a tongue depressor. The tongue depressors are placed into the boxes to identify the center in which each child will be working.

## B. Charts

Attach library book pockets to a firm sheet of tagboard. Place a child's name on each pocket. Print the names of the learning centers on card strips. The cards are placed into the pockets to indicate the learning center at which each child is to work.

| ART | MUSIC | MATH | READING | COOKING |
|-----|-------|------|---------|---------|
| JOE | MEG | Bob | HAL | PAM |
| JIM |  | Kim | SALLY | Ed |
|  |  |  | JAN | FLO |
|  |  |  |  |  |
|  |  |  |  |  |
|  |  |  |  |  |

Divide a firm sheet of tagboard into columns headed with the names of the learning center areas. Screw a number of cup hooks into each column. Make a cardboard name tag for each student. Punch a hole at the top. Name tags are placed on the hooks to indicate the center at which a child is to work.

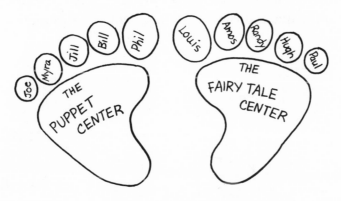

STEP TO THE LEARNING CENTERS

Cut footprint patterns out of tagboard and tape them to the wall, floor, or bulletin board. Print the names of the centers on the soles. Tape the children's names to the toes to indicate which centers they are to work in.

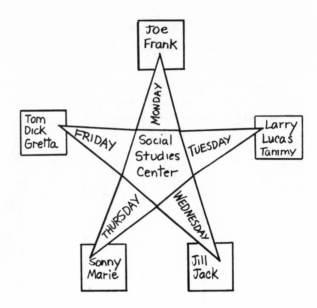

"Center Stars" can be used to schedule groups of children to various centers during each day of the week. Cut large stars from tagboard. Print the name of the center in the middle and the days of the week on the points. Mount the stars near the appropriate center. Each day, tape the names of the children to the appropriate points of the appropriate star.

Other attractive formats similar to "Center Stars" can be devised for making daily learning center assignments.

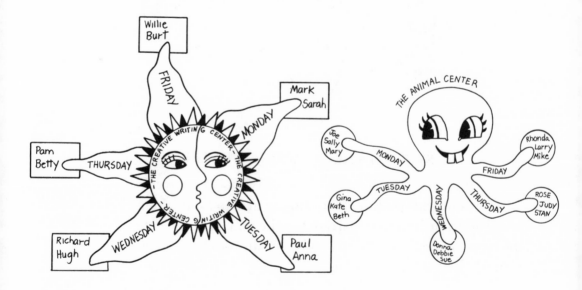

## C. Contracts

Contracts require the students to sign up for the activities with which they will be working each day. With young children, initially the contract form should include pictorial symbols which are coordinated with symbols placed near or on the learning center. Gradually, the contract forms may become more abstract. There are many formats that may be used for drawing contracts, but whatever the format, the important outcome is that the children gain a sense of responsibility for following a daily or weekly planning guide.

A very useful device is to use large beverage or ice cream containers as a "Post Office," assigning a section to each child as a mailbox. The teacher and students may leave personalized messages or contracts in the slots indicating the work to be done in each learning center.

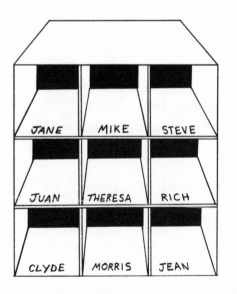

 HAPPY-GRAM

Dear Freddy,

I know you enjoy listening to exciting adventure stories and looking at books. The Listening Center has been reserved for you at 1:30 so that you can listen and read along with the new adventure story.

Various formats for contracts are illustrated on the pages that follow. The progression is from concrete to abstract representation of centers, and from limited to greater student choice of which center to work in and of activities within a center. Also, as children gain experience in choosing and completing activities, they may be given greater responsibility for organizing their own time.

An effective method for progressing from stong teacher guidance to the gradual use of free choice may follow these steps:

1.  Initially, you may wish to direct the children to all of the centers in which they are to work. *(See contracts 1 and 2.)*

2.  Next, you may wish to identify specific centers in which the children are required to work, but allow them to make one or two personal choices in addition. *(See contract 3.)*

3.  Next, using a contract that lists the activities within each center, you may assign children to specific centers, but give them the freedom to choose from among the activities contained in each center. *(See contracts 4 and 5.)*

4.  Ultimately, you may wish to allow children opportunities to freely plan their own activities and organize their own schedules. Such plans may initially be made for a period of one day and gradually be extended to an entire week or longer. *(See contracts 6 through 10.)*

When such progression has been followed, the classroom environment gradually becomes less teacher-centered, and the children begin to assume the major responsibility for their own learning.

## Contract 1

The teacher assigns the children to the centers they are to work in by coloring a balloon on each child's contract form. The child finds the appropriate center by matching the balloon color to the color code on the designated center.

*Contract 2*

The teacher calls out the center to which each child is assigned. The child colors the circle with crayon to identify the center to which he has been assigned. The centers are color coded.

*Contract 3*

The teacher puts checks in the circles to specify the one or two centers at which the child is to work. The child is then given freedom to make one or two free choices of additional centers she would like to work in. The Meeting Box is used to indicate a teacher- or pupil-initiated conference period.

*Contract 4*

The teacher assigns the centers at which the children are to work by placing an X in the appropriate circle. The children are free to choose the activities within each designated center. Each places an X on the activity chosen.

| ◯   SOCIAL STUDIES | ◯   READING |
|---|---|
| ◯ Map bingo | ◯ Word dominoes |
| ◯ Game board | ◯ Sound stories |
| ◯ Cross country trip | ◯ Sight word rummy |
| ◯ Map making | ◯ Word folders |
| ◯   WRITING | ◯   LISTENING |
| ◯ Practice sheets | ◯ Tape recorder |
| ◯ Sandbox writing | ◯ Sound cylinders |
| ◯ Story starters | ◯ Matching game |
| ◯ Typewriter | ◯ Follow the directions |
| Name _____ | |

## Contract 5

The children identify the activities they choose to do within the assigned centers by writing their selections on the window panes.

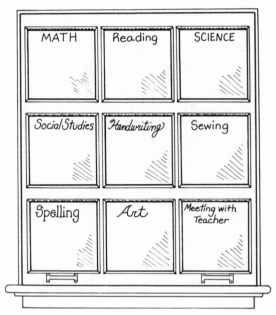

## Contract 6

This form may be used when learning centers occupy an entire day or a large block of time during the day. The children identify the activities they have chosen and establish their own time schedules for these activities. When they complete each activity they evaluate it.

| Daily Plan | | |
|---|---|---|
| Name: _____ Date: _____ | | |
| These are the activities I've planned for today. | | |
| Time | Activity | How I felt about what I did |
|  |  |  |
|  |  |  |
|  |  |  |
|  |  |  |

*Contract 7*

This form encourages children to extend their planning skills to the organization of a week-long schedule. The children choose the centers they will work on each day and record the time they plan to spend in these centers in the appropriate boxes on the contract.

| Name |  |  |  |  |  |
|---|---|---|---|---|---|
| Center | Monday | Tuesday | Wednesday | Thursday | Friday |
| Writing |  |  |  |  |  |
| SCIENCE |  |  |  |  |  |
| Reading |  |  |  |  |  |
| ART |  |  |  |  |  |
| Listening |  |  |  |  |  |

*Contract 8*

This form requires children to create a detailed schedule for a week's work. The children indicate what time they will work in the centers of their choice each day. They also indicate which activities in the center they will do. They may also add comments and evaluations about completed activities in the boxes.

Name _____

| Listening | Science | Math |
|---|---|---|
| Art | Reading | Cooking |
| Social Studies | Writing | Music |

| Time | Monday | Tuesday | Wednesday | Thursday | Friday |
|---|---|---|---|---|---|
|  |  |  |  |  |  |
|  |  |  |  |  |  |
|  |  |  |  |  |  |
|  |  |  |  |  |  |
|  |  |  |  |  |  |

*Contract 9*

This contract form and the one that follows—Contract 10—are especially useful for project-oriented learning centers. They call upon the children to make long-range commitments to complete work in the area of their chosen interests.

---

**CONTRACT**

I am interested in doing the following work in the
_____ learning center.

_____

_____

I will spend about _____ minutes each day in the center. It will take me about _____ days to finish my work.

**SEAL OF APPROVAL**

My signature

_____

---

*Contract 10*

Ye Olde Contract

I, _____, do hereby agree to work in
the _____ learning center and complete the activities and projects listed below. It will take me about _____ days to finish my work.

Activities and Projects:

☐ Charts and graphs

☐ Scrapbooks

☐ Cartoon or editorial

## Guiding Children in the Use of Learning Centers

1. Inform the students about how the learning centers are to be used. Don't get involved with detailed educational jargon, but explain these points simply:

- What kinds of activities are available at our centers?

- When are the centers to be used?

- How is each center to be used?

- How are the children to be assigned to the various centers?

- What responsibilities do the children who are working at the centers have?

- What is to be done with the work which has been completed?

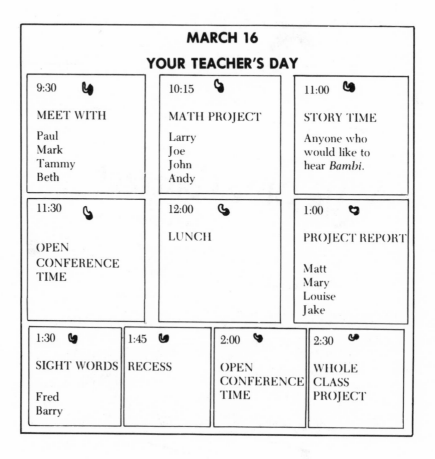

| | | |
|---|---|---|
| **MARCH 16** | | |
| **YOUR TEACHER'S DAY** | | |
| 9:30<br><br>MEET WITH<br>Paul<br>Mark<br>Tammy<br>Beth | 10:15<br><br>MATH PROJECT<br>Larry<br>Joe<br>John<br>Andy | 11:00<br><br>STORY TIME<br>Anyone who<br>would like to<br>hear *Bambi*. |
| 11:30<br><br>OPEN<br>CONFERENCE<br>TIME | 12:00<br><br>LUNCH | 1:00<br><br>PROJECT REPORT<br>Matt<br>Mary<br>Louise<br>Jake |
| 1:30<br><br>SIGHT WORDS<br><br>Fred<br>Barry | 1:45<br><br>RECESS | 2:00<br><br>OPEN<br>CONFERENCE<br>TIME |
| | | 2:30<br><br>WHOLE<br>CLASS<br>PROJECT |

2. Inform the children of your availability for the day. You will need to divide your time among activities such as: giving individual or group assistance, holding conferences, special teaching to small groups, guiding whole-group projects, etc. The children need to know when they may call upon you for help and when you should not be interrupted. Making your plans known to the children assists them in self-direction and in formulating their own plans for the day. The sample format on the opposite page utilizes heavy tagboard with cup hooks on which the teacher hangs cards indicating the schedule for the day.

## Evaluation and Record-keeping

"HOW CAN I EVER EXPECT TO KEEP TRACK
OF EACH CHILD'S WORK RECORD?"

Effective record-keeping is essential to the success of learning-center based instruction. With concise record-keeping forms, excessive paper work and hours of extensive review may be kept at a minimum. Forms of various design can be used to keep track of children's interests, involvement, skills, and deficiencies. Some of these forms may be completed by the children; others will have to be maintained by the teacher. Some sample checklists are presented here.

This checklist may be constructed as a large chart. It gives a quick picture of the centers in which each of your children has worked. As the children complete a center, they record the number of the center and the date on the chart.

| STUDENT | LEARNING CENTERS | | | |
|---|---|---|---|---|
| | MATH | SCIENCE | READING | ART |
| Morris | | | | |
| James | | | | |
| Matilda | | | | |
| Michelle | | | | |
| Gloria | | | | |
| Patrick | | | | |
| Glenda | | | | |
| McArthur | | | | |
| Blaine | | | | |

This checklist shows the teacher at a glance how many of the children have completed each specific learning center. Such format can provide the teacher with useful information about revisions or additions that may be needed in various curricular areas. The children record the date they worked in the specified centers on this chart.

| NAME | LEARNING CENTERS | | | |
|---|---|---|---|---|
| | INSECT GAME | MINIZOO | FOOD CHAINS | BUTTERFLY COLLECTION |
| Morris | | | | |
| James | | | | |
| Matilda | | | | |
| Michelle | | | | |
| Gloria | | | | |
| Patrick | | | | |
| Glenda | | | | |
| McArthur | | | | |

Various types of student record forms can be used to gather information about how meaningful, interesting, enjoyable, appropriate the children found the centers to be. Two sample special student checklists are presented.

Dear Teacher,

I colored the pictures for the things I did today. I circled the centers that I liked a lot.

SCIENCE

SPELLING

AQUARIUM

ART

READING

MATH

Name: _____ Date: _____

Another Day in the Life of . . .

_____.

Date:_____.

| Center | Activity | My Personal Reaction |
|--------|----------|----------------------|
|        |          |                      |
|        |          |                      |
|        |          |                      |
|        |          |                      |

Signed: _____

## "HOW EFFECTIVE WILL I BE
## WITH THIS NEW KIND OF CLASSROOM?"

Trying something new is always a bit frightening. But you will have many indications that tell you how effective you have been. You will know from your own and your children's reactions whether it has been an enjoyable experience. You will observe whether you are more relaxed, more stimulated, more excited about teaching. You will observe whether your children are more interested, more involved, happier in school.

You will know whether it has been a profitable experience. You will observe whether your children are developing proficiencies and skills in subject areas and whether they seem to be gaining in self-confidence, intitiative, and independence. You will know by their test scores, by comments from their parents, by their motivation, whether their achievement is the same, poorer, or better than it had been in a more formal learning environment.

Finally, you will judge the impact of this approach on specific individual children. You will know which ones flourish in an environment that encourages responsibility for self-learning, and which ones may need more structure, more instruction, more outer controls. Eventually, you will be able to design a classroom set-up that will be flexible enough to meet almost all your children's needs.

This book has presented and illustrated each of the major processes involved in learning-center teaching approaches. The challenge facing each of you is that of applying the suggestions to the unique situation in which you and your students find yourselves. Give this approach a chance—hopefully, you will experience a profound increase in motivation, enthusiasm, and independence in your students and also in yourself.

# SUGGESTED READINGS ON LEARNING CENTERS AND OPEN LEARNING

Barth, Roland S. *Open Education and the American School*. New York: Agathen Press, Inc., 1972.

Blackburn, Jack E. and Conrad Powell. *One at a Time All at Once*. Pacific Palisades, California: Goodyear Publishing Company, Inc., 1976.

Blitz, Barbara. *The Open Classroom: Making It Work*. Boston: Allyn and Bacon, Inc., 1973.

Blake, Howard E. *Creating a Learning-Centered Classroom*. New York: Hart Publishing Co., 1977.

Bremer, Anne and John Bremer. *Open Education: A Beginning*. New York: Holt, Rinehart and Winston, 1972.

Breyfogle, Ethel, et al. *Creating a Learning Environment: A Learning Center Handbook*. Santa Monica, California: Goodyear Publishing Company, Inc., 1976.

Chittenden, Edward A., et at. *Analysis of an Approach to Open Education*. Princeton, New Jersey: Educational Testing Service, 1970.

Davidson, Tom et al. *The Learning Center Book*. Pacific Palisades, California: Goodyear Publishing Company, Inc., 1976.

Day, Barbara. *Open Learning in Early Childhood*. New York: Macmillan Publishing Company, Inc., 1975.

Dunn, Rita and Kenneth Dunn. *Practical Approaches to Individualizing Instruction: Contracts and Other Effective Teaching Strategies*. West Nyack, New York: Parker Publishing Company, Inc., 1972.

Featherstone, Joseph. *Schools Where Children Learn*. New York: Liveright Publishing Corporation, 1971.

Fisk, Lori and Clay Lindgren. *Learning Centers*. Glen Ridge, New Jersey: Exceptional Press, 1974.

Forte, Imogene and Mary Ann Pangle. *Center Stuff for Nooks, Crannies and Corners*. Nashville, Tennessee: Incentive Publications, 1974.

Holt, John. *Freedom and Beyond*. New York: E.P. Dutton and Company, Inc., 1972.

Holt, John. *How Children Fail*. New York: Pitman Publishing Corporation, 1964.

Holt, John. *How Children Learn*. New York: Pitman Publishing Corporation, 1967.

Holt, John. *What Do I Do Monday?* New York: E.P. Dutton and Company, Inc., 1970.

Kahl, David H. and Barbara T. Gast. *Learning Centers in the Open Classroom*. Encino, California: International Center for Educational Development, 1974.

Kaplan, Sandra Nina, et al. *A Young Child Experiences*. Pacific Palisades, California: Goodyear Publishing Company, Inc., 1975.

Kaplan, Sandra Nina, et al. *Change For Children*. Pacific Palisades, California: Goodyear Publishing Company, Inc., 1973.

Kohl, Herbert R. *The Open Classroom*. New York: The New York Review, 1972.

Kohl, Herbert R. *The Open Classroom: A Practical Guide to a New Way of Teaching*. New York: Vintage Books, 1969.

Lloyd, Dorothy M. *70 Activities for Classroom Learning Centers*. Dansville, New York: The Instructor Publications, Inc., 1974.

Lorton, Mary Baratta. *Workjobs*. Reading, Massachusetts: Addison-Wesley Publishing Company, 1972.

Marzollo, Jean and Janice Lloyd. *Learning Through Play*. New York: Harper and Row, Publishers, 1972.

Miller, John P. *Humanizing the Classroom*. New York: Praeger Publishers, 1976.

Rathbone, Charles H., ed. *Open Education: The Informal Classroom*. New York: Citation Press, 1971.

Rogers, Vincent R. *Teaching in the British Primary School*. New York: Macmillan Publishing Company, Inc., 1970.

Seaberg, Dorothy I. *The Four Faces of Teaching*. Pacific Palisades, California: Goodyear Publishing Company, Inc., 1974.

Silberman, Charles E. *Crisis in the Classroom: The Remaking of American Education*. New York: Random House, Inc., 1970.

Silberman, Charles E., ed. *The Open Classroom Reader*. New York: Vintage Books, 1973.

Stafford, Gerald and Randall Pelow. *Getting Started With Learning Centers*. Minneapolis, Minnesota: Burgess Publishing Company, 1974.

Stephens, Lillian S. *The Teacher's Guide to Open Education*. New York: Holt, Rinehart and Winston, Inc., 1974.

Thomas, John I. *Learning Centers: Opening Up the Classroom*. Boston: Holbrook Press, Inc., 1975.

Voight, Ralph Claude. *Invitation to Learning: The Learning Center Handbook*. Washington, D.C.: Acropolis Books, Ltd., 1971.

Waynant, Louise F. and Robert M. Wilson. *Learning Centers ... A Guide for Effective Use*. Paoli, Pennsylvania: The Instructo Corporation, 1974.

Weber, Lillian. *The English Infant School and Informal Education*. Englewood Cliffs, New Jersey: Prentice-Hall, Inc., 1971.

Wurman, Richard Saul, ed. *Yellow Pages of Learning Resources*. Cambridge, Massachusetts: MIT Press, 1972.

**HART**

Some other titles in the Hart Education series:

**CREATING A LEARNING-CENTERED CLASSROOM:**
**A Practical Guide for Teachers**

HOWARD E. BLAKE

The traditional classroom consists of rows of children in rows of desks and a teacher up front teaching the same thing to all of them at the same time. When it became clear how unsatisfactory this approach was, alternative educational approaches were eagerly sought. The chief problem lay in building a humanistic environment in which children could thrive emotionally and socially, while concurrently teaching them needed academic skills and basic knowledge.

The learning-centered classroom does both.

In this book, Howard Blake tells the teacher exactly how to do it—how to choose a model, how to organize and manage the classroom, how to create interesting and appropriate learning centers, how to keep ongoing records of progress.

*400 pages.   Hardcover* **$12.50**.   *Paperback* **$7.95.**

## DEVELOPING EFFECTIVE CLASSROOM GROUPS:
## A Practical Guide for Teachers

GENE STANFORD

Every teacher who faces a class knows that whether it will be a good year or a bad year depends to a large extent on the group ambience. Over and above how dynamic the teacher is, or how fascinating the subject matter may be, is the learning climate. Many classes cannot get on with their work because discipline problems or interpersonal conflict are constantly disruptive. And many teachers feel helpless and hopeless about affecting the way in which the group members relate to each other.

In this book the teacher learns how to convert a class of individuals into an effective group. Dr. Stanford introduces the teacher to the strategies of group dynamics applicable to the classroom. The book is primarily a practical guide, with emphasis on specific things to do that will enhance learning, promote social growth, and ease tension and discipline problems. Described in detail are scores of practical techniques in the form of games and activities which will give students practice and experience in developing the skills of working together as a mature, effective group.

*160 pages.    Hardcover* **$10.00**.    *Paperback* **$4.95.**

## VALUES CLARIFICATION: A Handbook of Practical Strategies for Teachers and Students

SIDNEY B. SIMON, LELAND W. HOWE, HOWARD KIRSCHENBAUM

Designed to engage students and teachers in the active formulation and examination of values, this book is unique in content and format. It does not teach a particular set of values. There is no sermonizing or moralizing. The goal is to involve students in practical experiences, making them aware of *their own* feelings, *their own* ideas, *their own* beliefs, so that the choices and decisions they make are conscious and deliberate, based on *their own* value systems.

This important and relevant book presents numerous practical strategies which plunge student and teacher directly into the evaluating process. Students will find these activities intriguing, and closely related to their personal lives. Teachers will find the suggestions simple, practical, stimulating.

*397 pages. Hardcover* **$8.95**. *Paperback* **$4.95.**

## PERSONALIZING EDUCATION: Values Clarification and Beyond

LELAND W. HOWE and MARY MARTHA HOWE

Within a brief few years, values clarification has become an immensely popular teaching concept. The question now being raised, both by critics and supporters, is whether values clarification is a fad, or is a teaching tool that will continue to be useful.

The Howes believe that values clarification may indeed fade away in the coming decade unless teachers regard the technique as an integral part of the classroom: a way of thinking about teaching, a way of relating to students, a way of *personalizing* education so that every student can achieve his full potential.

What are the really useful methods for personalizing education and how does a teacher use them? These are the primary questions this book answers. Here are techniques for personalizing (1) human relationships, (2) goals in the classroom, (3) the curriculum, and (4) classroom organization and management, plus well over 100 strategies and worksheets.

*448 pages.    Hardcover* **$10.00**.   *Paperback* **$5.95.**